**UNIVERSITY OF MOUNT UNION
LIBRARY**

MT UNION CURRIC CENTER

Division Facts
Practice Book

Improve Your Math Fluency Series

Chris McMullen, Ph.D.

WITHDRAWN
UNIV OF MOUNT UNION LIBRARY

Division Facts Practice Book
Improve Your Math Fluency Series

Copyright (c) 2009 Chris McMullen, Ph.D.

All rights reserved. This includes the right to reproduce any portion of this book in any form. However, teachers who purchase one copy of this book, or borrow one physical copy from a library, may make and distribute photocopies of selected pages for instructional purposes for their own classes only. Also, parents who purchase one copy of this book, or borrow one physical copy from a library, may make and distribute photocopies of selected pages for use by their own children only.

CreateSpace

Nonfiction / Education / Elementary School
Professional & Technical / Education / Specific Skills / Mathematics
Children's / Science / Mathematics

ISBN: 1448609755

EAN-13: 9781448609758

Contents

Multiplication Table

	1	2	3	4	5	6	7	8	9	10
1	1	2	3	4	5	6	7	8	9	10
2	2	4	6	8	10	12	14	16	18	20
3	3	6	9	12	15	18	21	24	27	30
4	4	8	12	16	20	24	28	32	36	40
5	5	10	15	20	25	30	35	40	45	50
6	6	12	18	24	30	36	42	48	54	60
7	7	14	21	28	35	42	49	56	63	70
8	8	16	24	32	40	48	56	64	72	80
9	9	18	27	36	45	54	63	72	81	90
10	10	20	30	40	50	60	70	80	90	100

Making the Most of this Workbook

- Mathematics is a language. You can't hold a decent conversation in any language if you have a limited vocabulary or if you are not fluent. In order to become successful in mathematics, you need to practice until you have mastered the fundamentals and developed fluency in the subject. This *Division Facts Practice Book* will help you improve your division skills.

- You may need to consult the multiplication table on page 4 occasionally as you begin your practice, but should refrain from relying on it. Force yourself to solve the problems independently as much as possible. It is necessary to memorize the basic division facts and know them quickly in order to become successful at division.

- Use Part 1 of this book to practice memorizing the basic division facts and to learn them quickly. Each page in Part 1 features a single number.

- Part 2 of this book will help you focus on dividing numbers where the divisor is no larger than 5. This way you are not challenged with too much at once.

- Concentrate on problems where the divisor is greater than 5 in Part 3 of this book.

- Part 4 of this book includes all division facts with divisor and quotient between 0 and 10 mixed together. You are ready to move onto Part 4 when you can complete the practice pages of Parts 2 and 3 quickly with few mistakes. Part 4 will help you develop fluency in your knowledge of division facts.

- After you complete a page, check your answers with a calculator. Practice makes permanent, but not necessarily perfect: If you practice making mistakes, you will learn your mistakes. Check your answers and learn from your mistakes such that you practice solving the problems correctly. This way your practice will make perfect.

- Math can be fun. Make a game of your practice by recording your times and trying to improve on your times, and recording your scores and trying to improve on your scores. Doing this will help you see how much you are improving, and this sign of improvement can give you the confidence to succeed in math, which can help you learn to enjoy this subject more.

Part 1: Practice Individual Division Facts

Time: _____   Score: _____

$0 \div 1 =$	$4 \div 1 =$	$10 \div 1 =$	$5 \div 1 =$
$0 \div 1 =$	$9 \div 1 =$	$5 \div 1 =$	$0 \div 1 =$
$2 \div 1 =$	$0 \div 1 =$	$4 \div 1 =$	$1 \div 1 =$
$10 \div 1 =$	$8 \div 1 =$	$4 \div 1 =$	$10 \div 1 =$
$0 \div 1 =$	$4 \div 1 =$	$8 \div 1 =$	$1 \div 1 =$
$2 \div 1 =$	$9 \div 1 =$	$0 \div 1 =$	$9 \div 1 =$
$0 \div 1 =$	$3 \div 1 =$	$6 \div 1 =$	$4 \div 1 =$
$3 \div 1 =$	$5 \div 1 =$	$7 \div 1 =$	$8 \div 1 =$
$7 \div 1 =$	$10 \div 1 =$	$3 \div 1 =$	$10 \div 1 =$
$5 \div 1 =$	$10 \div 1 =$	$8 \div 1 =$	$4 \div 1 =$
$0 \div 1 =$	$8 \div 1 =$	$10 \div 1 =$	$6 \div 1 =$
$4 \div 1 =$	$7 \div 1 =$	$10 \div 1 =$	$8 \div 1 =$
$6 \div 1 =$	$10 \div 1 =$	$8 \div 1 =$	$5 \div 1 =$
$4 \div 1 =$	$3 \div 1 =$	$5 \div 1 =$	$9 \div 1 =$
$0 \div 1 =$	$9 \div 1 =$	$4 \div 1 =$	$1 \div 1 =$
$9 \div 1 =$	$3 \div 1 =$	$4 \div 1 =$	$8 \div 1 =$
$0 \div 1 =$	$2 \div 1 =$	$5 \div 1 =$	$3 \div 1 =$

Time: _____   Score: _____

2 ÷ 1 =	10 ÷ 1 =	5 ÷ 1 =	3 ÷ 1 =
9 ÷ 1 =	2 ÷ 1 =	7 ÷ 1 =	0 ÷ 1 =
2 ÷ 1 =	3 ÷ 1 =	5 ÷ 1 =	9 ÷ 1 =
4 ÷ 1 =	10 ÷ 1 =	3 ÷ 1 =	6 ÷ 1 =
0 ÷ 1 =	4 ÷ 1 =	3 ÷ 1 =	8 ÷ 1 =
10 ÷ 1 =	2 ÷ 1 =	10 ÷ 1 =	2 ÷ 1 =
8 ÷ 1 =	1 ÷ 1 =	4 ÷ 1 =	2 ÷ 1 =
10 ÷ 1 =	9 ÷ 1 =	0 ÷ 1 =	6 ÷ 1 =
7 ÷ 1 =	9 ÷ 1 =	3 ÷ 1 =	8 ÷ 1 =
6 ÷ 1 =	4 ÷ 1 =	10 ÷ 1 =	1 ÷ 1 =
7 ÷ 1 =	8 ÷ 1 =	0 ÷ 1 =	1 ÷ 1 =
2 ÷ 1 =	0 ÷ 1 =	1 ÷ 1 =	3 ÷ 1 =
6 ÷ 1 =	9 ÷ 1 =	7 ÷ 1 =	3 ÷ 1 =
7 ÷ 1 =	9 ÷ 1 =	8 ÷ 1 =	2 ÷ 1 =
0 ÷ 1 =	3 ÷ 1 =	6 ÷ 1 =	8 ÷ 1 =
1 ÷ 1 =	0 ÷ 1 =	3 ÷ 1 =	8 ÷ 1 =
5 ÷ 1 =	9 ÷ 1 =	0 ÷ 1 =	2 ÷ 1 =
9 ÷ 1 =	7 ÷ 1 =	2 ÷ 1 =	6 ÷ 1 =

Time: _____   Score: _____

$9 \div 1 =$	$8 \div 1 =$	$4 \div 1 =$	$7 \div 1 =$
$8 \div 1 =$	$9 \div 1 =$	$8 \div 1 =$	$9 \div 1 =$
$7 \div 1 =$	$3 \div 1 =$	$2 \div 1 =$	$5 \div 1 =$
$10 \div 1 =$	$3 \div 1 =$	$10 \div 1 =$	$6 \div 1 =$
$2 \div 1 =$	$8 \div 1 =$	$2 \div 1 =$	$7 \div 1 =$
$5 \div 1 =$	$9 \div 1 =$	$10 \div 1 =$	$4 \div 1 =$
$7 \div 1 =$	$0 \div 1 =$	$7 \div 1 =$	$0 \div 1 =$
$1 \div 1 =$	$2 \div 1 =$	$1 \div 1 =$	$0 \div 1 =$
$4 \div 1 =$	$7 \div 1 =$	$0 \div 1 =$	$4 \div 1 =$
$9 \div 1 =$	$2 \div 1 =$	$1 \div 1 =$	$3 \div 1 =$
$3 \div 1 =$	$7 \div 1 =$	$4 \div 1 =$	$5 \div 1 =$
$8 \div 1 =$	$3 \div 1 =$	$9 \div 1 =$	$8 \div 1 =$
$9 \div 1 =$	$5 \div 1 =$	$0 \div 1 =$	$1 \div 1 =$
$4 \div 1 =$	$7 \div 1 =$	$10 \div 1 =$	$8 \div 1 =$
$10 \div 1 =$	$9 \div 1 =$	$10 \div 1 =$	$2 \div 1 =$
$7 \div 1 =$	$8 \div 1 =$	$7 \div 1 =$	$2 \div 1 =$
$8 \div 1 =$	$9 \div 1 =$	$4 \div 1 =$	$1 \div 1 =$
$5 \div 1 =$	$0 \div 1 =$	$10 \div 1 =$	$1 \div 1 =$

Time: _____

Score: _____

6 ÷ 1 =	4 ÷ 1 =	7 ÷ 1 =	1 ÷ 1 =
5 ÷ 1 =	9 ÷ 1 =	10 ÷ 1 =	5 ÷ 1 =
9 ÷ 1 =	5 ÷ 1 =	3 ÷ 1 =	5 ÷ 1 =
1 ÷ 1 =	2 ÷ 1 =	10 ÷ 1 =	2 ÷ 1 =
9 ÷ 1 =	8 ÷ 1 =	10 ÷ 1 =	7 ÷ 1 =
10 ÷ 1 =	1 ÷ 1 =	5 ÷ 1 =	3 ÷ 1 =
4 ÷ 1 =	2 ÷ 1 =	0 ÷ 1 =	1 ÷ 1 =
2 ÷ 1 =	1 ÷ 1 =	7 ÷ 1 =	10 ÷ 1 =
10 ÷ 1 =	7 ÷ 1 =	10 ÷ 1 =	6 ÷ 1 =
7 ÷ 1 =	9 ÷ 1 =	8 ÷ 1 =	3 ÷ 1 =
9 ÷ 1 =	2 ÷ 1 =	10 ÷ 1 =	0 ÷ 1 =
5 ÷ 1 =	10 ÷ 1 =	8 ÷ 1 =	0 ÷ 1 =
7 ÷ 1 =	8 ÷ 1 =	5 ÷ 1 =	9 ÷ 1 =
1 ÷ 1 =	0 ÷ 1 =	10 ÷ 1 =	3 ÷ 1 =
0 ÷ 1 =	5 ÷ 1 =	1 ÷ 1 =	4 ÷ 1 =
3 ÷ 1 =	0 ÷ 1 =	8 ÷ 1 =	10 ÷ 1 =
0 ÷ 1 =	5 ÷ 1 =	6 ÷ 1 =	0 ÷ 1 =
8 ÷ 1 =	4 ÷ 1 =	6 ÷ 1 =	4 ÷ 1 =

Time: _____   Score: _____

$0 \div 2 =$	$8 \div 2 =$	$6 \div 2 =$	$18 \div 2 =$
$12 \div 2 =$	$6 \div 2 =$	$8 \div 2 =$	$18 \div 2 =$
$12 \div 2 =$	$18 \div 2 =$	$8 \div 2 =$	$0 \div 2 =$
$12 \div 2 =$	$10 \div 2 =$	$8 \div 2 =$	$10 \div 2 =$
$14 \div 2 =$	$4 \div 2 =$	$14 \div 2 =$	$4 \div 2 =$
$0 \div 2 =$	$6 \div 2 =$	$14 \div 2 =$	$4 \div 2 =$
$18 \div 2 =$	$16 \div 2 =$	$4 \div 2 =$	$12 \div 2 =$
$18 \div 2 =$	$4 \div 2 =$	$8 \div 2 =$	$20 \div 2 =$
$18 \div 2 =$	$20 \div 2 =$	$4 \div 2 =$	$8 \div 2 =$
$16 \div 2 =$	$14 \div 2 =$	$18 \div 2 =$	$4 \div 2 =$
$16 \div 2 =$	$12 \div 2 =$	$6 \div 2 =$	$20 \div 2 =$
$6 \div 2 =$	$14 \div 2 =$	$8 \div 2 =$	$6 \div 2 =$
$18 \div 2 =$	$20 \div 2 =$	$18 \div 2 =$	$10 \div 2 =$
$12 \div 2 =$	$0 \div 2 =$	$18 \div 2 =$	$12 \div 2 =$
$16 \div 2 =$	$6 \div 2 =$	$0 \div 2 =$	$4 \div 2 =$
$16 \div 2 =$	$12 \div 2 =$	$16 \div 2 =$	$14 \div 2 =$
$2 \div 2 =$	$6 \div 2 =$	$20 \div 2 =$	$6 \div 2 =$
$0 \div 2 =$	$12 \div 2 =$	$16 \div 2 =$	$18 \div 2 =$

Division Facts Practice Book

Time: _____   Score: _____

14 ÷ 2 =	4 ÷ 2 =	12 ÷ 2 =	20 ÷ 2 =
14 ÷ 2 =	18 ÷ 2 =	2 ÷ 2 =	16 ÷ 2 =
6 ÷ 2 =	8 ÷ 2 =	16 ÷ 2 =	6 ÷ 2 =
18 ÷ 2 =	20 ÷ 2 =	18 ÷ 2 =	10 ÷ 2 =
16 ÷ 2 =	6 ÷ 2 =	8 ÷ 2 =	6 ÷ 2 =
10 ÷ 2 =	14 ÷ 2 =	8 ÷ 2 =	2 ÷ 2 =
2 ÷ 2 =	14 ÷ 2 =	10 ÷ 2 =	16 ÷ 2 =
8 ÷ 2 =	4 ÷ 2 =	18 ÷ 2 =	2 ÷ 2 =
0 ÷ 2 =	18 ÷ 2 =	4 ÷ 2 =	6 ÷ 2 =
12 ÷ 2 =	4 ÷ 2 =	18 ÷ 2 =	10 ÷ 2 =
14 ÷ 2 =	2 ÷ 2 =	18 ÷ 2 =	14 ÷ 2 =
6 ÷ 2 =	20 ÷ 2 =	10 ÷ 2 =	2 ÷ 2 =
12 ÷ 2 =	16 ÷ 2 =	12 ÷ 2 =	14 ÷ 2 =
16 ÷ 2 =	14 ÷ 2 =	16 ÷ 2 =	20 ÷ 2 =
4 ÷ 2 =	10 ÷ 2 =	6 ÷ 2 =	20 ÷ 2 =
0 ÷ 2 =	12 ÷ 2 =	20 ÷ 2 =	2 ÷ 2 =
8 ÷ 2 =	2 ÷ 2 =	10 ÷ 2 =	14 ÷ 2 =
12 ÷ 2 =	18 ÷ 2 =	10 ÷ 2 =	2 ÷ 2 =

Time: _____   Score: _____

$18 \div 2 =$	$6 \div 2 =$	$2 \div 2 =$	$8 \div 2 =$
$16 \div 2 =$	$0 \div 2 =$	$2 \div 2 =$	$14 \div 2 =$
$0 \div 2 =$	$20 \div 2 =$	$12 \div 2 =$	$8 \div 2 =$
$10 \div 2 =$	$20 \div 2 =$	$18 \div 2 =$	$4 \div 2 =$
$12 \div 2 =$	$6 \div 2 =$	$14 \div 2 =$	$2 \div 2 =$
$18 \div 2 =$	$10 \div 2 =$	$12 \div 2 =$	$6 \div 2 =$
$20 \div 2 =$	$0 \div 2 =$	$16 \div 2 =$	$4 \div 2 =$
$20 \div 2 =$	$12 \div 2 =$	$16 \div 2 =$	$20 \div 2 =$
$6 \div 2 =$	$14 \div 2 =$	$8 \div 2 =$	$4 \div 2 =$
$20 \div 2 =$	$14 \div 2 =$	$20 \div 2 =$	$8 \div 2 =$
$20 \div 2 =$	$4 \div 2 =$	$2 \div 2 =$	$4 \div 2 =$
$2 \div 2 =$	$18 \div 2 =$	$10 \div 2 =$	$16 \div 2 =$
$2 \div 2 =$	$14 \div 2 =$	$12 \div 2 =$	$8 \div 2 =$
$14 \div 2 =$	$4 \div 2 =$	$14 \div 2 =$	$12 \div 2 =$
$14 \div 2 =$	$8 \div 2 =$	$2 \div 2 =$	$0 \div 2 =$
$20 \div 2 =$	$8 \div 2 =$	$6 \div 2 =$	$0 \div 2 =$
$18 \div 2 =$	$6 \div 2 =$	$20 \div 2 =$	$6 \div 2 =$
$10 \div 2 =$	$14 \div 2 =$	$18 \div 2 =$	$0 \div 2 =$

Time: _____   Score: _____

4 ÷ 2 =	14 ÷ 2 =	12 ÷ 2 =	10 ÷ 2 =
0 ÷ 2 =	4 ÷ 2 =	16 ÷ 2 =	2 ÷ 2 =
16 ÷ 2 =	0 ÷ 2 =	2 ÷ 2 =	0 ÷ 2 =
2 ÷ 2 =	0 ÷ 2 =	12 ÷ 2 =	10 ÷ 2 =
14 ÷ 2 =	8 ÷ 2 =	14 ÷ 2 =	2 ÷ 2 =
0 ÷ 2 =	14 ÷ 2 =	18 ÷ 2 =	20 ÷ 2 =
0 ÷ 2 =	2 ÷ 2 =	14 ÷ 2 =	0 ÷ 2 =
8 ÷ 2 =	18 ÷ 2 =	16 ÷ 2 =	6 ÷ 2 =
0 ÷ 2 =	10 ÷ 2 =	12 ÷ 2 =	10 ÷ 2 =
14 ÷ 2 =	18 ÷ 2 =	2 ÷ 2 =	0 ÷ 2 =
2 ÷ 2 =	14 ÷ 2 =	8 ÷ 2 =	6 ÷ 2 =
18 ÷ 2 =	6 ÷ 2 =	4 ÷ 2 =	2 ÷ 2 =
0 ÷ 2 =	16 ÷ 2 =	6 ÷ 2 =	20 ÷ 2 =
16 ÷ 2 =	2 ÷ 2 =	16 ÷ 2 =	2 ÷ 2 =
2 ÷ 2 =	16 ÷ 2 =	6 ÷ 2 =	8 ÷ 2 =
14 ÷ 2 =	12 ÷ 2 =	18 ÷ 2 =	8 ÷ 2 =
14 ÷ 2 =	20 ÷ 2 =	18 ÷ 2 =	8 ÷ 2 =
16 ÷ 2 =	6 ÷ 2 =	2 ÷ 2 =	0 ÷ 2 =

Time: _____   Score: _____

3 ÷ 3 =	24 ÷ 3 =	18 ÷ 3 =	12 ÷ 3 =
18 ÷ 3 =	6 ÷ 3 =	0 ÷ 3 =	18 ÷ 3 =
27 ÷ 3 =	24 ÷ 3 =	15 ÷ 3 =	3 ÷ 3 =
24 ÷ 3 =	9 ÷ 3 =	21 ÷ 3 =	6 ÷ 3 =
6 ÷ 3 =	24 ÷ 3 =	21 ÷ 3 =	30 ÷ 3 =
18 ÷ 3 =	24 ÷ 3 =	9 ÷ 3 =	6 ÷ 3 =
27 ÷ 3 =	30 ÷ 3 =	27 ÷ 3 =	15 ÷ 3 =
3 ÷ 3 =	30 ÷ 3 =	6 ÷ 3 =	21 ÷ 3 =
24 ÷ 3 =	0 ÷ 3 =	21 ÷ 3 =	12 ÷ 3 =
3 ÷ 3 =	6 ÷ 3 =	21 ÷ 3 =	6 ÷ 3 =
12 ÷ 3 =	27 ÷ 3 =	3 ÷ 3 =	6 ÷ 3 =
0 ÷ 3 =	27 ÷ 3 =	12 ÷ 3 =	0 ÷ 3 =
6 ÷ 3 =	30 ÷ 3 =	18 ÷ 3 =	21 ÷ 3 =
0 ÷ 3 =	9 ÷ 3 =	6 ÷ 3 =	27 ÷ 3 =
21 ÷ 3 =	9 ÷ 3 =	18 ÷ 3 =	9 ÷ 3 =
15 ÷ 3 =	6 ÷ 3 =	15 ÷ 3 =	18 ÷ 3 =
6 ÷ 3 =	9 ÷ 3 =	15 ÷ 3 =	27 ÷ 3 =
15 ÷ 3 =	24 ÷ 3 =	6 ÷ 3 =	15 ÷ 3 =

Time: _____   Score: _____

24 ÷ 3 =	3 ÷ 3 =	30 ÷ 3 =	15 ÷ 3 =
24 ÷ 3 =	9 ÷ 3 =	15 ÷ 3 =	27 ÷ 3 =
0 ÷ 3 =	12 ÷ 3 =	30 ÷ 3 =	3 ÷ 3 =
15 ÷ 3 =	12 ÷ 3 =	24 ÷ 3 =	27 ÷ 3 =
27 ÷ 3 =	21 ÷ 3 =	24 ÷ 3 =	27 ÷ 3 =
12 ÷ 3 =	0 ÷ 3 =	21 ÷ 3 =	3 ÷ 3 =
15 ÷ 3 =	12 ÷ 3 =	0 ÷ 3 =	6 ÷ 3 =
24 ÷ 3 =	21 ÷ 3 =	24 ÷ 3 =	15 ÷ 3 =
21 ÷ 3 =	6 ÷ 3 =	18 ÷ 3 =	0 ÷ 3 =
6 ÷ 3 =	18 ÷ 3 =	30 ÷ 3 =	18 ÷ 3 =
9 ÷ 3 =	30 ÷ 3 =	0 ÷ 3 =	12 ÷ 3 =
30 ÷ 3 =	15 ÷ 3 =	3 ÷ 3 =	15 ÷ 3 =
30 ÷ 3 =	0 ÷ 3 =	30 ÷ 3 =	0 ÷ 3 =
9 ÷ 3 =	15 ÷ 3 =	21 ÷ 3 =	18 ÷ 3 =
24 ÷ 3 =	0 ÷ 3 =	18 ÷ 3 =	9 ÷ 3 =
30 ÷ 3 =	0 ÷ 3 =	18 ÷ 3 =	12 ÷ 3 =
30 ÷ 3 =	15 ÷ 3 =	18 ÷ 3 =	12 ÷ 3 =
21 ÷ 3 =	9 ÷ 3 =	15 ÷ 3 =	24 ÷ 3 =

Time: _____   Score: _____

3 ÷ 3 =	18 ÷ 3 =	12 ÷ 3 =	24 ÷ 3 =
21 ÷ 3 =	9 ÷ 3 =	21 ÷ 3 =	18 ÷ 3 =
0 ÷ 3 =	3 ÷ 3 =	12 ÷ 3 =	6 ÷ 3 =
9 ÷ 3 =	24 ÷ 3 =	12 ÷ 3 =	15 ÷ 3 =
18 ÷ 3 =	0 ÷ 3 =	24 ÷ 3 =	18 ÷ 3 =
12 ÷ 3 =	27 ÷ 3 =	3 ÷ 3 =	27 ÷ 3 =
6 ÷ 3 =	3 ÷ 3 =	27 ÷ 3 =	21 ÷ 3 =
24 ÷ 3 =	3 ÷ 3 =	27 ÷ 3 =	18 ÷ 3 =
24 ÷ 3 =	21 ÷ 3 =	0 ÷ 3 =	9 ÷ 3 =
6 ÷ 3 =	24 ÷ 3 =	30 ÷ 3 =	24 ÷ 3 =
9 ÷ 3 =	30 ÷ 3 =	15 ÷ 3 =	9 ÷ 3 =
30 ÷ 3 =	15 ÷ 3 =	12 ÷ 3 =	15 ÷ 3 =
24 ÷ 3 =	9 ÷ 3 =	15 ÷ 3 =	30 ÷ 3 =
6 ÷ 3 =	15 ÷ 3 =	12 ÷ 3 =	24 ÷ 3 =
0 ÷ 3 =	6 ÷ 3 =	9 ÷ 3 =	18 ÷ 3 =
12 ÷ 3 =	27 ÷ 3 =	6 ÷ 3 =	0 ÷ 3 =
0 ÷ 3 =	6 ÷ 3 =	24 ÷ 3 =	21 ÷ 3 =
6 ÷ 3 =	30 ÷ 3 =	27 ÷ 3 =	12 ÷ 3 =

Time: _____   Score: _____

0 ÷ 3 =	9 ÷ 3 =	0 ÷ 3 =	9 ÷ 3 =
30 ÷ 3 =	18 ÷ 3 =	3 ÷ 3 =	15 ÷ 3 =
24 ÷ 3 =	0 ÷ 3 =	9 ÷ 3 =	12 ÷ 3 =
15 ÷ 3 =	18 ÷ 3 =	30 ÷ 3 =	12 ÷ 3 =
18 ÷ 3 =	3 ÷ 3 =	18 ÷ 3 =	30 ÷ 3 =
15 ÷ 3 =	9 ÷ 3 =	3 ÷ 3 =	9 ÷ 3 =
15 ÷ 3 =	6 ÷ 3 =	30 ÷ 3 =	15 ÷ 3 =
27 ÷ 3 =	21 ÷ 3 =	9 ÷ 3 =	18 ÷ 3 =
24 ÷ 3 =	6 ÷ 3 =	21 ÷ 3 =	30 ÷ 3 =
3 ÷ 3 =	27 ÷ 3 =	18 ÷ 3 =	3 ÷ 3 =
9 ÷ 3 =	15 ÷ 3 =	21 ÷ 3 =	0 ÷ 3 =
9 ÷ 3 =	6 ÷ 3 =	30 ÷ 3 =	0 ÷ 3 =
0 ÷ 3 =	9 ÷ 3 =	30 ÷ 3 =	9 ÷ 3 =
21 ÷ 3 =	3 ÷ 3 =	21 ÷ 3 =	18 ÷ 3 =
30 ÷ 3 =	27 ÷ 3 =	18 ÷ 3 =	24 ÷ 3 =
3 ÷ 3 =	0 ÷ 3 =	12 ÷ 3 =	9 ÷ 3 =
12 ÷ 3 =	24 ÷ 3 =	18 ÷ 3 =	12 ÷ 3 =
6 ÷ 3 =	30 ÷ 3 =	24 ÷ 3 =	15 ÷ 3 =

Time: _____   Score: _____

$36 \div 4 =$	$32 \div 4 =$	$20 \div 4 =$	$4 \div 4 =$
$0 \div 4 =$	$8 \div 4 =$	$12 \div 4 =$	$36 \div 4 =$
$4 \div 4 =$	$16 \div 4 =$	$4 \div 4 =$	$16 \div 4 =$
$40 \div 4 =$	$12 \div 4 =$	$8 \div 4 =$	$20 \div 4 =$
$28 \div 4 =$	$36 \div 4 =$	$4 \div 4 =$	$8 \div 4 =$
$40 \div 4 =$	$12 \div 4 =$	$0 \div 4 =$	$12 \div 4 =$
$0 \div 4 =$	$4 \div 4 =$	$36 \div 4 =$	$16 \div 4 =$
$32 \div 4 =$	$4 \div 4 =$	$12 \div 4 =$	$8 \div 4 =$
$40 \div 4 =$	$0 \div 4 =$	$12 \div 4 =$	$36 \div 4 =$
$40 \div 4 =$	$12 \div 4 =$	$40 \div 4 =$	$20 \div 4 =$
$4 \div 4 =$	$24 \div 4 =$	$28 \div 4 =$	$16 \div 4 =$
$20 \div 4 =$	$28 \div 4 =$	$20 \div 4 =$	$12 \div 4 =$
$20 \div 4 =$	$16 \div 4 =$	$4 \div 4 =$	$0 \div 4 =$
$32 \div 4 =$	$28 \div 4 =$	$8 \div 4 =$	$0 \div 4 =$
$4 \div 4 =$	$8 \div 4 =$	$24 \div 4 =$	$0 \div 4 =$
$4 \div 4 =$	$0 \div 4 =$	$24 \div 4 =$	$40 \div 4 =$
$16 \div 4 =$	$28 \div 4 =$	$32 \div 4 =$	$28 \div 4 =$
$36 \div 4 =$	$40 \div 4 =$	$32 \div 4 =$	$4 \div 4 =$

Time: _____   Score: _____

4 ÷ 4 =	12 ÷ 4 =	4 ÷ 4 =	32 ÷ 4 =
24 ÷ 4 =	0 ÷ 4 =	40 ÷ 4 =	4 ÷ 4 =
12 ÷ 4 =	0 ÷ 4 =	32 ÷ 4 =	40 ÷ 4 =
0 ÷ 4 =	28 ÷ 4 =	20 ÷ 4 =	28 ÷ 4 =
20 ÷ 4 =	0 ÷ 4 =	28 ÷ 4 =	0 ÷ 4 =
40 ÷ 4 =	28 ÷ 4 =	0 ÷ 4 =	28 ÷ 4 =
36 ÷ 4 =	8 ÷ 4 =	20 ÷ 4 =	4 ÷ 4 =
12 ÷ 4 =	4 ÷ 4 =	32 ÷ 4 =	40 ÷ 4 =
0 ÷ 4 =	24 ÷ 4 =	32 ÷ 4 =	24 ÷ 4 =
36 ÷ 4 =	12 ÷ 4 =	0 ÷ 4 =	24 ÷ 4 =
4 ÷ 4 =	12 ÷ 4 =	8 ÷ 4 =	28 ÷ 4 =
40 ÷ 4 =	24 ÷ 4 =	12 ÷ 4 =	32 ÷ 4 =
36 ÷ 4 =	32 ÷ 4 =	28 ÷ 4 =	16 ÷ 4 =
40 ÷ 4 =	20 ÷ 4 =	4 ÷ 4 =	24 ÷ 4 =
28 ÷ 4 =	36 ÷ 4 =	40 ÷ 4 =	12 ÷ 4 =
4 ÷ 4 =	20 ÷ 4 =	40 ÷ 4 =	8 ÷ 4 =
32 ÷ 4 =	16 ÷ 4 =	32 ÷ 4 =	36 ÷ 4 =
20 ÷ 4 =	32 ÷ 4 =	24 ÷ 4 =	16 ÷ 4 =

Time: _____   Score: _____

$16 \div 4 =$	$0 \div 4 =$	$12 \div 4 =$	$0 \div 4 =$
$24 \div 4 =$	$0 \div 4 =$	$28 \div 4 =$	$8 \div 4 =$
$8 \div 4 =$	$4 \div 4 =$	$20 \div 4 =$	$28 \div 4 =$
$8 \div 4 =$	$40 \div 4 =$	$8 \div 4 =$	$36 \div 4 =$
$40 \div 4 =$	$8 \div 4 =$	$36 \div 4 =$	$12 \div 4 =$
$24 \div 4 =$	$16 \div 4 =$	$12 \div 4 =$	$0 \div 4 =$
$36 \div 4 =$	$12 \div 4 =$	$16 \div 4 =$	$0 \div 4 =$
$20 \div 4 =$	$40 \div 4 =$	$24 \div 4 =$	$16 \div 4 =$
$16 \div 4 =$	$36 \div 4 =$	$8 \div 4 =$	$20 \div 4 =$
$16 \div 4 =$	$24 \div 4 =$	$16 \div 4 =$	$24 \div 4 =$
$36 \div 4 =$	$12 \div 4 =$	$0 \div 4 =$	$40 \div 4 =$
$16 \div 4 =$	$28 \div 4 =$	$40 \div 4 =$	$20 \div 4 =$
$0 \div 4 =$	$8 \div 4 =$	$16 \div 4 =$	$8 \div 4 =$
$24 \div 4 =$	$16 \div 4 =$	$40 \div 4 =$	$24 \div 4 =$
$4 \div 4 =$	$40 \div 4 =$	$32 \div 4 =$	$0 \div 4 =$
$8 \div 4 =$	$16 \div 4 =$	$24 \div 4 =$	$16 \div 4 =$
$20 \div 4 =$	$12 \div 4 =$	$4 \div 4 =$	$20 \div 4 =$
$12 \div 4 =$	$36 \div 4 =$	$24 \div 4 =$	$36 \div 4 =$

Time: _____   Score: _____

0 ÷ 4 =	28 ÷ 4 =	12 ÷ 4 =	8 ÷ 4 =
12 ÷ 4 =	20 ÷ 4 =	32 ÷ 4 =	40 ÷ 4 =
28 ÷ 4 =	12 ÷ 4 =	20 ÷ 4 =	16 ÷ 4 =
24 ÷ 4 =	12 ÷ 4 =	24 ÷ 4 =	28 ÷ 4 =
40 ÷ 4 =	36 ÷ 4 =	16 ÷ 4 =	0 ÷ 4 =
24 ÷ 4 =	8 ÷ 4 =	28 ÷ 4 =	36 ÷ 4 =
40 ÷ 4 =	36 ÷ 4 =	32 ÷ 4 =	28 ÷ 4 =
16 ÷ 4 =	36 ÷ 4 =	0 ÷ 4 =	4 ÷ 4 =
28 ÷ 4 =	0 ÷ 4 =	32 ÷ 4 =	40 ÷ 4 =
32 ÷ 4 =	40 ÷ 4 =	20 ÷ 4 =	0 ÷ 4 =
0 ÷ 4 =	32 ÷ 4 =	20 ÷ 4 =	8 ÷ 4 =
0 ÷ 4 =	16 ÷ 4 =	0 ÷ 4 =	32 ÷ 4 =
20 ÷ 4 =	24 ÷ 4 =	4 ÷ 4 =	20 ÷ 4 =
0 ÷ 4 =	16 ÷ 4 =	24 ÷ 4 =	16 ÷ 4 =
24 ÷ 4 =	28 ÷ 4 =	32 ÷ 4 =	20 ÷ 4 =
24 ÷ 4 =	36 ÷ 4 =	28 ÷ 4 =	12 ÷ 4 =
36 ÷ 4 =	8 ÷ 4 =	20 ÷ 4 =	28 ÷ 4 =
32 ÷ 4 =	40 ÷ 4 =	32 ÷ 4 =	4 ÷ 4 =

Time: _____   Score: _____

20 ÷ 5 =	30 ÷ 5 =	35 ÷ 5 =	10 ÷ 5 =
20 ÷ 5 =	15 ÷ 5 =	0 ÷ 5 =	45 ÷ 5 =
40 ÷ 5 =	10 ÷ 5 =	0 ÷ 5 =	5 ÷ 5 =
45 ÷ 5 =	50 ÷ 5 =	10 ÷ 5 =	25 ÷ 5 =
10 ÷ 5 =	30 ÷ 5 =	0 ÷ 5 =	5 ÷ 5 =
10 ÷ 5 =	5 ÷ 5 =	20 ÷ 5 =	5 ÷ 5 =
20 ÷ 5 =	50 ÷ 5 =	20 ÷ 5 =	35 ÷ 5 =
5 ÷ 5 =	40 ÷ 5 =	30 ÷ 5 =	10 ÷ 5 =
5 ÷ 5 =	10 ÷ 5 =	30 ÷ 5 =	0 ÷ 5 =
5 ÷ 5 =	10 ÷ 5 =	50 ÷ 5 =	25 ÷ 5 =
35 ÷ 5 =	45 ÷ 5 =	10 ÷ 5 =	25 ÷ 5 =
20 ÷ 5 =	10 ÷ 5 =	45 ÷ 5 =	15 ÷ 5 =
5 ÷ 5 =	40 ÷ 5 =	5 ÷ 5 =	30 ÷ 5 =
10 ÷ 5 =	25 ÷ 5 =	10 ÷ 5 =	35 ÷ 5 =
20 ÷ 5 =	0 ÷ 5 =	10 ÷ 5 =	45 ÷ 5 =
50 ÷ 5 =	0 ÷ 5 =	10 ÷ 5 =	35 ÷ 5 =
35 ÷ 5 =	30 ÷ 5 =	50 ÷ 5 =	10 ÷ 5 =
20 ÷ 5 =	10 ÷ 5 =	45 ÷ 5 =	50 ÷ 5 =

Time: _____   Score: _____

25 ÷ 5 =	50 ÷ 5 =	10 ÷ 5 =	15 ÷ 5 =
30 ÷ 5 =	40 ÷ 5 =	30 ÷ 5 =	5 ÷ 5 =
30 ÷ 5 =	20 ÷ 5 =	30 ÷ 5 =	40 ÷ 5 =
25 ÷ 5 =	5 ÷ 5 =	35 ÷ 5 =	0 ÷ 5 =
10 ÷ 5 =	20 ÷ 5 =	30 ÷ 5 =	5 ÷ 5 =
15 ÷ 5 =	10 ÷ 5 =	20 ÷ 5 =	30 ÷ 5 =
40 ÷ 5 =	15 ÷ 5 =	5 ÷ 5 =	10 ÷ 5 =
50 ÷ 5 =	40 ÷ 5 =	15 ÷ 5 =	5 ÷ 5 =
50 ÷ 5 =	45 ÷ 5 =	25 ÷ 5 =	15 ÷ 5 =
30 ÷ 5 =	20 ÷ 5 =	25 ÷ 5 =	35 ÷ 5 =
30 ÷ 5 =	0 ÷ 5 =	50 ÷ 5 =	25 ÷ 5 =
10 ÷ 5 =	0 ÷ 5 =	50 ÷ 5 =	45 ÷ 5 =
20 ÷ 5 =	15 ÷ 5 =	50 ÷ 5 =	5 ÷ 5 =
35 ÷ 5 =	15 ÷ 5 =	35 ÷ 5 =	40 ÷ 5 =
15 ÷ 5 =	0 ÷ 5 =	20 ÷ 5 =	15 ÷ 5 =
0 ÷ 5 =	40 ÷ 5 =	20 ÷ 5 =	45 ÷ 5 =
10 ÷ 5 =	15 ÷ 5 =	30 ÷ 5 =	40 ÷ 5 =
45 ÷ 5 =	10 ÷ 5 =	50 ÷ 5 =	35 ÷ 5 =

Time: _____   Score: _____

$35 \div 5 =$	$50 \div 5 =$	$25 \div 5 =$	$35 \div 5 =$
$0 \div 5 =$	$5 \div 5 =$	$45 \div 5 =$	$35 \div 5 =$
$30 \div 5 =$	$25 \div 5 =$	$45 \div 5 =$	$0 \div 5 =$
$45 \div 5 =$	$35 \div 5 =$	$0 \div 5 =$	$30 \div 5 =$
$15 \div 5 =$	$0 \div 5 =$	$35 \div 5 =$	$45 \div 5 =$
$40 \div 5 =$	$10 \div 5 =$	$35 \div 5 =$	$20 \div 5 =$
$30 \div 5 =$	$40 \div 5 =$	$45 \div 5 =$	$35 \div 5 =$
$40 \div 5 =$	$10 \div 5 =$	$25 \div 5 =$	$0 \div 5 =$
$10 \div 5 =$	$20 \div 5 =$	$15 \div 5 =$	$40 \div 5 =$
$35 \div 5 =$	$40 \div 5 =$	$45 \div 5 =$	$35 \div 5 =$
$45 \div 5 =$	$25 \div 5 =$	$35 \div 5 =$	$20 \div 5 =$
$0 \div 5 =$	$35 \div 5 =$	$10 \div 5 =$	$30 \div 5 =$
$30 \div 5 =$	$50 \div 5 =$	$20 \div 5 =$	$0 \div 5 =$
$35 \div 5 =$	$15 \div 5 =$	$30 \div 5 =$	$50 \div 5 =$
$35 \div 5 =$	$0 \div 5 =$	$10 \div 5 =$	$20 \div 5 =$
$40 \div 5 =$	$30 \div 5 =$	$10 \div 5 =$	$45 \div 5 =$
$35 \div 5 =$	$10 \div 5 =$	$25 \div 5 =$	$20 \div 5 =$
$35 \div 5 =$	$10 \div 5 =$	$50 \div 5 =$	$45 \div 5 =$

Time: _____   Score: _____

$20 \div 5 =$	$50 \div 5 =$	$25 \div 5 =$	$40 \div 5 =$
$10 \div 5 =$	$35 \div 5 =$	$25 \div 5 =$	$20 \div 5 =$
$25 \div 5 =$	$10 \div 5 =$	$30 \div 5 =$	$10 \div 5 =$
$35 \div 5 =$	$45 \div 5 =$	$20 \div 5 =$	$35 \div 5 =$
$20 \div 5 =$	$25 \div 5 =$	$15 \div 5 =$	$45 \div 5 =$
$40 \div 5 =$	$20 \div 5 =$	$30 \div 5 =$	$45 \div 5 =$
$30 \div 5 =$	$0 \div 5 =$	$20 \div 5 =$	$30 \div 5 =$
$40 \div 5 =$	$35 \div 5 =$	$15 \div 5 =$	$30 \div 5 =$
$40 \div 5 =$	$20 \div 5 =$	$25 \div 5 =$	$20 \div 5 =$
$50 \div 5 =$	$30 \div 5 =$	$40 \div 5 =$	$45 \div 5 =$
$35 \div 5 =$	$50 \div 5 =$	$0 \div 5 =$	$40 \div 5 =$
$0 \div 5 =$	$35 \div 5 =$	$5 \div 5 =$	$45 \div 5 =$
$0 \div 5 =$	$40 \div 5 =$	$35 \div 5 =$	$40 \div 5 =$
$25 \div 5 =$	$45 \div 5 =$	$35 \div 5 =$	$5 \div 5 =$
$15 \div 5 =$	$30 \div 5 =$	$50 \div 5 =$	$40 \div 5 =$
$5 \div 5 =$	$50 \div 5 =$	$20 \div 5 =$	$5 \div 5 =$
$10 \div 5 =$	$45 \div 5 =$	$50 \div 5 =$	$25 \div 5 =$
$30 \div 5 =$	$5 \div 5 =$	$45 \div 5 =$	$15 \div 5 =$

Time: _____   Score: _____

48 ÷ 6 =	36 ÷ 6 =	12 ÷ 6 =	24 ÷ 6 =
54 ÷ 6 =	24 ÷ 6 =	12 ÷ 6 =	48 ÷ 6 =
0 ÷ 6 =	60 ÷ 6 =	24 ÷ 6 =	0 ÷ 6 =
24 ÷ 6 =	12 ÷ 6 =	18 ÷ 6 =	54 ÷ 6 =
24 ÷ 6 =	12 ÷ 6 =	42 ÷ 6 =	6 ÷ 6 =
0 ÷ 6 =	60 ÷ 6 =	0 ÷ 6 =	36 ÷ 6 =
42 ÷ 6 =	36 ÷ 6 =	18 ÷ 6 =	12 ÷ 6 =
6 ÷ 6 =	54 ÷ 6 =	30 ÷ 6 =	36 ÷ 6 =
36 ÷ 6 =	30 ÷ 6 =	36 ÷ 6 =	54 ÷ 6 =
18 ÷ 6 =	60 ÷ 6 =	12 ÷ 6 =	48 ÷ 6 =
12 ÷ 6 =	0 ÷ 6 =	30 ÷ 6 =	42 ÷ 6 =
30 ÷ 6 =	60 ÷ 6 =	12 ÷ 6 =	48 ÷ 6 =
42 ÷ 6 =	24 ÷ 6 =	48 ÷ 6 =	60 ÷ 6 =
12 ÷ 6 =	42 ÷ 6 =	12 ÷ 6 =	36 ÷ 6 =
60 ÷ 6 =	6 ÷ 6 =	0 ÷ 6 =	60 ÷ 6 =
0 ÷ 6 =	6 ÷ 6 =	24 ÷ 6 =	60 ÷ 6 =
24 ÷ 6 =	18 ÷ 6 =	30 ÷ 6 =	48 ÷ 6 =
18 ÷ 6 =	30 ÷ 6 =	36 ÷ 6 =	48 ÷ 6 =

Time: _____   Score: _____

0 ÷ 6 =	24 ÷ 6 =	48 ÷ 6 =	6 ÷ 6 =
12 ÷ 6 =	42 ÷ 6 =	60 ÷ 6 =	0 ÷ 6 =
12 ÷ 6 =	18 ÷ 6 =	6 ÷ 6 =	42 ÷ 6 =
30 ÷ 6 =	0 ÷ 6 =	24 ÷ 6 =	54 ÷ 6 =
24 ÷ 6 =	0 ÷ 6 =	24 ÷ 6 =	30 ÷ 6 =
0 ÷ 6 =	24 ÷ 6 =	60 ÷ 6 =	36 ÷ 6 =
48 ÷ 6 =	60 ÷ 6 =	18 ÷ 6 =	54 ÷ 6 =
48 ÷ 6 =	36 ÷ 6 =	54 ÷ 6 =	60 ÷ 6 =
30 ÷ 6 =	24 ÷ 6 =	60 ÷ 6 =	24 ÷ 6 =
60 ÷ 6 =	54 ÷ 6 =	60 ÷ 6 =	18 ÷ 6 =
48 ÷ 6 =	30 ÷ 6 =	36 ÷ 6 =	24 ÷ 6 =
36 ÷ 6 =	24 ÷ 6 =	42 ÷ 6 =	54 ÷ 6 =
54 ÷ 6 =	60 ÷ 6 =	24 ÷ 6 =	18 ÷ 6 =
36 ÷ 6 =	6 ÷ 6 =	60 ÷ 6 =	42 ÷ 6 =
54 ÷ 6 =	12 ÷ 6 =	36 ÷ 6 =	18 ÷ 6 =
36 ÷ 6 =	42 ÷ 6 =	54 ÷ 6 =	60 ÷ 6 =
18 ÷ 6 =	48 ÷ 6 =	12 ÷ 6 =	60 ÷ 6 =
18 ÷ 6 =	6 ÷ 6 =	36 ÷ 6 =	6 ÷ 6 =

Time: _____   Score: _____

30 ÷ 6 =	6 ÷ 6 =	12 ÷ 6 =	54 ÷ 6 =
0 ÷ 6 =	30 ÷ 6 =	18 ÷ 6 =	6 ÷ 6 =
12 ÷ 6 =	0 ÷ 6 =	42 ÷ 6 =	24 ÷ 6 =
18 ÷ 6 =	24 ÷ 6 =	12 ÷ 6 =	24 ÷ 6 =
60 ÷ 6 =	54 ÷ 6 =	48 ÷ 6 =	18 ÷ 6 =
0 ÷ 6 =	18 ÷ 6 =	42 ÷ 6 =	6 ÷ 6 =
12 ÷ 6 =	54 ÷ 6 =	0 ÷ 6 =	60 ÷ 6 =
48 ÷ 6 =	36 ÷ 6 =	12 ÷ 6 =	18 ÷ 6 =
24 ÷ 6 =	54 ÷ 6 =	24 ÷ 6 =	12 ÷ 6 =
0 ÷ 6 =	30 ÷ 6 =	18 ÷ 6 =	12 ÷ 6 =
42 ÷ 6 =	18 ÷ 6 =	12 ÷ 6 =	6 ÷ 6 =
18 ÷ 6 =	0 ÷ 6 =	12 ÷ 6 =	48 ÷ 6 =
24 ÷ 6 =	6 ÷ 6 =	30 ÷ 6 =	18 ÷ 6 =
36 ÷ 6 =	24 ÷ 6 =	0 ÷ 6 =	42 ÷ 6 =
6 ÷ 6 =	48 ÷ 6 =	60 ÷ 6 =	36 ÷ 6 =
18 ÷ 6 =	54 ÷ 6 =	0 ÷ 6 =	54 ÷ 6 =
54 ÷ 6 =	0 ÷ 6 =	12 ÷ 6 =	60 ÷ 6 =
48 ÷ 6 =	18 ÷ 6 =	12 ÷ 6 =	36 ÷ 6 =

Time: _____   Score: _____

24 ÷ 6 =	36 ÷ 6 =	18 ÷ 6 =	54 ÷ 6 =
12 ÷ 6 =	30 ÷ 6 =	0 ÷ 6 =	36 ÷ 6 =
18 ÷ 6 =	42 ÷ 6 =	6 ÷ 6 =	42 ÷ 6 =
24 ÷ 6 =	18 ÷ 6 =	42 ÷ 6 =	54 ÷ 6 =
30 ÷ 6 =	54 ÷ 6 =	18 ÷ 6 =	30 ÷ 6 =
42 ÷ 6 =	48 ÷ 6 =	24 ÷ 6 =	36 ÷ 6 =
48 ÷ 6 =	6 ÷ 6 =	60 ÷ 6 =	24 ÷ 6 =
18 ÷ 6 =	48 ÷ 6 =	54 ÷ 6 =	12 ÷ 6 =
6 ÷ 6 =	18 ÷ 6 =	60 ÷ 6 =	36 ÷ 6 =
54 ÷ 6 =	60 ÷ 6 =	36 ÷ 6 =	24 ÷ 6 =
36 ÷ 6 =	54 ÷ 6 =	12 ÷ 6 =	0 ÷ 6 =
6 ÷ 6 =	0 ÷ 6 =	60 ÷ 6 =	36 ÷ 6 =
12 ÷ 6 =	24 ÷ 6 =	0 ÷ 6 =	18 ÷ 6 =
12 ÷ 6 =	36 ÷ 6 =	12 ÷ 6 =	54 ÷ 6 =
48 ÷ 6 =	0 ÷ 6 =	60 ÷ 6 =	24 ÷ 6 =
54 ÷ 6 =	12 ÷ 6 =	48 ÷ 6 =	6 ÷ 6 =
30 ÷ 6 =	18 ÷ 6 =	12 ÷ 6 =	42 ÷ 6 =
60 ÷ 6 =	30 ÷ 6 =	48 ÷ 6 =	6 ÷ 6 =

Time: _____   Score: _____

$56 \div 7 =$	$70 \div 7 =$	$42 \div 7 =$	$70 \div 7 =$
$0 \div 7 =$	$28 \div 7 =$	$21 \div 7 =$	$28 \div 7 =$
$35 \div 7 =$	$49 \div 7 =$	$70 \div 7 =$	$35 \div 7 =$
$14 \div 7 =$	$0 \div 7 =$	$35 \div 7 =$	$0 \div 7 =$
$49 \div 7 =$	$21 \div 7 =$	$42 \div 7 =$	$49 \div 7 =$
$35 \div 7 =$	$56 \div 7 =$	$70 \div 7 =$	$49 \div 7 =$
$14 \div 7 =$	$63 \div 7 =$	$35 \div 7 =$	$0 \div 7 =$
$70 \div 7 =$	$7 \div 7 =$	$49 \div 7 =$	$63 \div 7 =$
$7 \div 7 =$	$70 \div 7 =$	$42 \div 7 =$	$35 \div 7 =$
$0 \div 7 =$	$42 \div 7 =$	$28 \div 7 =$	$14 \div 7 =$
$56 \div 7 =$	$0 \div 7 =$	$42 \div 7 =$	$7 \div 7 =$
$70 \div 7 =$	$42 \div 7 =$	$0 \div 7 =$	$70 \div 7 =$
$35 \div 7 =$	$70 \div 7 =$	$0 \div 7 =$	$63 \div 7 =$
$70 \div 7 =$	$56 \div 7 =$	$63 \div 7 =$	$42 \div 7 =$
$49 \div 7 =$	$42 \div 7 =$	$21 \div 7 =$	$0 \div 7 =$
$35 \div 7 =$	$7 \div 7 =$	$28 \div 7 =$	$14 \div 7 =$
$42 \div 7 =$	$56 \div 7 =$	$42 \div 7 =$	$35 \div 7 =$
$21 \div 7 =$	$14 \div 7 =$	$7 \div 7 =$	$49 \div 7 =$

Time: _____   Score: _____

42 ÷ 7 =	63 ÷ 7 =	56 ÷ 7 =	35 ÷ 7 =
63 ÷ 7 =	0 ÷ 7 =	28 ÷ 7 =	21 ÷ 7 =
14 ÷ 7 =	49 ÷ 7 =	35 ÷ 7 =	49 ÷ 7 =
14 ÷ 7 =	28 ÷ 7 =	63 ÷ 7 =	56 ÷ 7 =
49 ÷ 7 =	42 ÷ 7 =	35 ÷ 7 =	70 ÷ 7 =
49 ÷ 7 =	14 ÷ 7 =	42 ÷ 7 =	70 ÷ 7 =
7 ÷ 7 =	49 ÷ 7 =	42 ÷ 7 =	35 ÷ 7 =
21 ÷ 7 =	70 ÷ 7 =	42 ÷ 7 =	63 ÷ 7 =
14 ÷ 7 =	21 ÷ 7 =	0 ÷ 7 =	7 ÷ 7 =
21 ÷ 7 =	70 ÷ 7 =	42 ÷ 7 =	56 ÷ 7 =
7 ÷ 7 =	35 ÷ 7 =	7 ÷ 7 =	63 ÷ 7 =
14 ÷ 7 =	0 ÷ 7 =	63 ÷ 7 =	21 ÷ 7 =
49 ÷ 7 =	56 ÷ 7 =	42 ÷ 7 =	7 ÷ 7 =
63 ÷ 7 =	28 ÷ 7 =	21 ÷ 7 =	14 ÷ 7 =
21 ÷ 7 =	14 ÷ 7 =	35 ÷ 7 =	49 ÷ 7 =
7 ÷ 7 =	49 ÷ 7 =	70 ÷ 7 =	7 ÷ 7 =
56 ÷ 7 =	63 ÷ 7 =	35 ÷ 7 =	0 ÷ 7 =
14 ÷ 7 =	21 ÷ 7 =	28 ÷ 7 =	35 ÷ 7 =

Time: _____   Score: _____

$42 \div 7 =$	$28 \div 7 =$	$7 \div 7 =$	$70 \div 7 =$
$63 \div 7 =$	$14 \div 7 =$	$49 \div 7 =$	$35 \div 7 =$
$21 \div 7 =$	$49 \div 7 =$	$14 \div 7 =$	$0 \div 7 =$
$28 \div 7 =$	$42 \div 7 =$	$49 \div 7 =$	$14 \div 7 =$
$70 \div 7 =$	$63 \div 7 =$	$14 \div 7 =$	$21 \div 7 =$
$7 \div 7 =$	$63 \div 7 =$	$7 \div 7 =$	$0 \div 7 =$
$21 \div 7 =$	$7 \div 7 =$	$49 \div 7 =$	$63 \div 7 =$
$42 \div 7 =$	$21 \div 7 =$	$63 \div 7 =$	$21 \div 7 =$
$56 \div 7 =$	$7 \div 7 =$	$56 \div 7 =$	$49 \div 7 =$
$63 \div 7 =$	$7 \div 7 =$	$49 \div 7 =$	$70 \div 7 =$
$14 \div 7 =$	$70 \div 7 =$	$49 \div 7 =$	$14 \div 7 =$
$28 \div 7 =$	$21 \div 7 =$	$14 \div 7 =$	$35 \div 7 =$
$56 \div 7 =$	$42 \div 7 =$	$21 \div 7 =$	$49 \div 7 =$
$63 \div 7 =$	$0 \div 7 =$	$70 \div 7 =$	$28 \div 7 =$
$7 \div 7 =$	$35 \div 7 =$	$7 \div 7 =$	$35 \div 7 =$
$42 \div 7 =$	$70 \div 7 =$	$21 \div 7 =$	$49 \div 7 =$
$42 \div 7 =$	$7 \div 7 =$	$56 \div 7 =$	$28 \div 7 =$
$49 \div 7 =$	$56 \div 7 =$	$70 \div 7 =$	$35 \div 7 =$

Time: _____   Score: _____

70 ÷ 7 =	7 ÷ 7 =	14 ÷ 7 =	0 ÷ 7 =
49 ÷ 7 =	63 ÷ 7 =	28 ÷ 7 =	35 ÷ 7 =
14 ÷ 7 =	0 ÷ 7 =	35 ÷ 7 =	14 ÷ 7 =
28 ÷ 7 =	49 ÷ 7 =	7 ÷ 7 =	0 ÷ 7 =
42 ÷ 7 =	7 ÷ 7 =	28 ÷ 7 =	21 ÷ 7 =
49 ÷ 7 =	7 ÷ 7 =	0 ÷ 7 =	49 ÷ 7 =
70 ÷ 7 =	49 ÷ 7 =	63 ÷ 7 =	56 ÷ 7 =
0 ÷ 7 =	56 ÷ 7 =	0 ÷ 7 =	14 ÷ 7 =
7 ÷ 7 =	21 ÷ 7 =	63 ÷ 7 =	42 ÷ 7 =
56 ÷ 7 =	49 ÷ 7 =	28 ÷ 7 =	63 ÷ 7 =
49 ÷ 7 =	35 ÷ 7 =	49 ÷ 7 =	70 ÷ 7 =
14 ÷ 7 =	56 ÷ 7 =	0 ÷ 7 =	7 ÷ 7 =
63 ÷ 7 =	49 ÷ 7 =	56 ÷ 7 =	21 ÷ 7 =
0 ÷ 7 =	7 ÷ 7 =	63 ÷ 7 =	0 ÷ 7 =
49 ÷ 7 =	70 ÷ 7 =	14 ÷ 7 =	7 ÷ 7 =
56 ÷ 7 =	28 ÷ 7 =	42 ÷ 7 =	56 ÷ 7 =
35 ÷ 7 =	7 ÷ 7 =	14 ÷ 7 =	21 ÷ 7 =
28 ÷ 7 =	56 ÷ 7 =	0 ÷ 7 =	28 ÷ 7 =

Time: _____   Score: _____

$64 \div 8 =$	$16 \div 8 =$	$32 \div 8 =$	$16 \div 8 =$
$24 \div 8 =$	$48 \div 8 =$	$64 \div 8 =$	$16 \div 8 =$
$16 \div 8 =$	$56 \div 8 =$	$24 \div 8 =$	$80 \div 8 =$
$48 \div 8 =$	$40 \div 8 =$	$72 \div 8 =$	$32 \div 8 =$
$40 \div 8 =$	$72 \div 8 =$	$24 \div 8 =$	$64 \div 8 =$
$48 \div 8 =$	$56 \div 8 =$	$32 \div 8 =$	$64 \div 8 =$
$64 \div 8 =$	$40 \div 8 =$	$64 \div 8 =$	$56 \div 8 =$
$24 \div 8 =$	$32 \div 8 =$	$56 \div 8 =$	$80 \div 8 =$
$48 \div 8 =$	$80 \div 8 =$	$0 \div 8 =$	$64 \div 8 =$
$80 \div 8 =$	$32 \div 8 =$	$24 \div 8 =$	$16 \div 8 =$
$72 \div 8 =$	$40 \div 8 =$	$48 \div 8 =$	$32 \div 8 =$
$48 \div 8 =$	$16 \div 8 =$	$0 \div 8 =$	$40 \div 8 =$
$16 \div 8 =$	$40 \div 8 =$	$24 \div 8 =$	$56 \div 8 =$
$80 \div 8 =$	$56 \div 8 =$	$72 \div 8 =$	$8 \div 8 =$
$56 \div 8 =$	$64 \div 8 =$	$48 \div 8 =$	$56 \div 8 =$
$72 \div 8 =$	$48 \div 8 =$	$64 \div 8 =$	$80 \div 8 =$
$64 \div 8 =$	$80 \div 8 =$	$16 \div 8 =$	$0 \div 8 =$
$80 \div 8 =$	$40 \div 8 =$	$16 \div 8 =$	$32 \div 8 =$

Time: _____   Score: _____

48 ÷ 8 =	32 ÷ 8 =	48 ÷ 8 =	32 ÷ 8 =
16 ÷ 8 =	48 ÷ 8 =	64 ÷ 8 =	48 ÷ 8 =
16 ÷ 8 =	32 ÷ 8 =	16 ÷ 8 =	32 ÷ 8 =
72 ÷ 8 =	64 ÷ 8 =	56 ÷ 8 =	8 ÷ 8 =
64 ÷ 8 =	0 ÷ 8 =	24 ÷ 8 =	40 ÷ 8 =
0 ÷ 8 =	56 ÷ 8 =	48 ÷ 8 =	56 ÷ 8 =
48 ÷ 8 =	32 ÷ 8 =	56 ÷ 8 =	80 ÷ 8 =
0 ÷ 8 =	72 ÷ 8 =	8 ÷ 8 =	32 ÷ 8 =
8 ÷ 8 =	48 ÷ 8 =	64 ÷ 8 =	48 ÷ 8 =
56 ÷ 8 =	32 ÷ 8 =	40 ÷ 8 =	80 ÷ 8 =
32 ÷ 8 =	8 ÷ 8 =	72 ÷ 8 =	64 ÷ 8 =
16 ÷ 8 =	56 ÷ 8 =	80 ÷ 8 =	24 ÷ 8 =
48 ÷ 8 =	16 ÷ 8 =	24 ÷ 8 =	16 ÷ 8 =
0 ÷ 8 =	32 ÷ 8 =	80 ÷ 8 =	64 ÷ 8 =
80 ÷ 8 =	40 ÷ 8 =	48 ÷ 8 =	16 ÷ 8 =
56 ÷ 8 =	64 ÷ 8 =	16 ÷ 8 =	24 ÷ 8 =
0 ÷ 8 =	8 ÷ 8 =	24 ÷ 8 =	72 ÷ 8 =
24 ÷ 8 =	8 ÷ 8 =	24 ÷ 8 =	40 ÷ 8 =

Time: _____   Score: _____

$24 \div 8 =$	$40 \div 8 =$	$8 \div 8 =$	$40 \div 8 =$
$16 \div 8 =$	$72 \div 8 =$	$24 \div 8 =$	$56 \div 8 =$
$56 \div 8 =$	$0 \div 8 =$	$64 \div 8 =$	$8 \div 8 =$
$16 \div 8 =$	$8 \div 8 =$	$72 \div 8 =$	$48 \div 8 =$
$8 \div 8 =$	$48 \div 8 =$	$56 \div 8 =$	$32 \div 8 =$
$40 \div 8 =$	$8 \div 8 =$	$32 \div 8 =$	$0 \div 8 =$
$48 \div 8 =$	$80 \div 8 =$	$16 \div 8 =$	$32 \div 8 =$
$0 \div 8 =$	$24 \div 8 =$	$48 \div 8 =$	$0 \div 8 =$
$48 \div 8 =$	$56 \div 8 =$	$72 \div 8 =$	$64 \div 8 =$
$56 \div 8 =$	$64 \div 8 =$	$0 \div 8 =$	$48 \div 8 =$
$16 \div 8 =$	$40 \div 8 =$	$48 \div 8 =$	$80 \div 8 =$
$24 \div 8 =$	$48 \div 8 =$	$16 \div 8 =$	$56 \div 8 =$
$56 \div 8 =$	$24 \div 8 =$	$48 \div 8 =$	$32 \div 8 =$
$48 \div 8 =$	$32 \div 8 =$	$64 \div 8 =$	$24 \div 8 =$
$40 \div 8 =$	$48 \div 8 =$	$72 \div 8 =$	$40 \div 8 =$
$8 \div 8 =$	$48 \div 8 =$	$64 \div 8 =$	$40 \div 8 =$
$0 \div 8 =$	$16 \div 8 =$	$56 \div 8 =$	$80 \div 8 =$
$48 \div 8 =$	$80 \div 8 =$	$48 \div 8 =$	$56 \div 8 =$

Time: _____   Score: _____

0 ÷ 8 =	32 ÷ 8 =	72 ÷ 8 =	0 ÷ 8 =
40 ÷ 8 =	48 ÷ 8 =	64 ÷ 8 =	72 ÷ 8 =
72 ÷ 8 =	16 ÷ 8 =	40 ÷ 8 =	16 ÷ 8 =
24 ÷ 8 =	32 ÷ 8 =	0 ÷ 8 =	32 ÷ 8 =
72 ÷ 8 =	24 ÷ 8 =	80 ÷ 8 =	48 ÷ 8 =
32 ÷ 8 =	48 ÷ 8 =	56 ÷ 8 =	72 ÷ 8 =
40 ÷ 8 =	80 ÷ 8 =	64 ÷ 8 =	32 ÷ 8 =
16 ÷ 8 =	8 ÷ 8 =	32 ÷ 8 =	72 ÷ 8 =
16 ÷ 8 =	64 ÷ 8 =	40 ÷ 8 =	80 ÷ 8 =
8 ÷ 8 =	40 ÷ 8 =	0 ÷ 8 =	56 ÷ 8 =
24 ÷ 8 =	72 ÷ 8 =	48 ÷ 8 =	32 ÷ 8 =
56 ÷ 8 =	64 ÷ 8 =	32 ÷ 8 =	64 ÷ 8 =
0 ÷ 8 =	24 ÷ 8 =	8 ÷ 8 =	24 ÷ 8 =
56 ÷ 8 =	32 ÷ 8 =	40 ÷ 8 =	32 ÷ 8 =
80 ÷ 8 =	56 ÷ 8 =	24 ÷ 8 =	16 ÷ 8 =
80 ÷ 8 =	8 ÷ 8 =	0 ÷ 8 =	48 ÷ 8 =
72 ÷ 8 =	32 ÷ 8 =	48 ÷ 8 =	80 ÷ 8 =
16 ÷ 8 =	48 ÷ 8 =	64 ÷ 8 =	72 ÷ 8 =

Time: _____   Score: _____

45 ÷ 9 =	9 ÷ 9 =	36 ÷ 9 =	45 ÷ 9 =
81 ÷ 9 =	72 ÷ 9 =	18 ÷ 9 =	72 ÷ 9 =
36 ÷ 9 =	0 ÷ 9 =	81 ÷ 9 =	90 ÷ 9 =
9 ÷ 9 =	72 ÷ 9 =	36 ÷ 9 =	27 ÷ 9 =
54 ÷ 9 =	81 ÷ 9 =	54 ÷ 9 =	0 ÷ 9 =
36 ÷ 9 =	81 ÷ 9 =	63 ÷ 9 =	54 ÷ 9 =
90 ÷ 9 =	18 ÷ 9 =	36 ÷ 9 =	90 ÷ 9 =
81 ÷ 9 =	90 ÷ 9 =	45 ÷ 9 =	27 ÷ 9 =
9 ÷ 9 =	27 ÷ 9 =	18 ÷ 9 =	36 ÷ 9 =
18 ÷ 9 =	54 ÷ 9 =	63 ÷ 9 =	36 ÷ 9 =
54 ÷ 9 =	90 ÷ 9 =	27 ÷ 9 =	45 ÷ 9 =
18 ÷ 9 =	72 ÷ 9 =	36 ÷ 9 =	54 ÷ 9 =
0 ÷ 9 =	18 ÷ 9 =	0 ÷ 9 =	90 ÷ 9 =
18 ÷ 9 =	63 ÷ 9 =	72 ÷ 9 =	18 ÷ 9 =
63 ÷ 9 =	45 ÷ 9 =	36 ÷ 9 =	72 ÷ 9 =
27 ÷ 9 =	63 ÷ 9 =	72 ÷ 9 =	54 ÷ 9 =
36 ÷ 9 =	90 ÷ 9 =	63 ÷ 9 =	36 ÷ 9 =
27 ÷ 9 =	72 ÷ 9 =	9 ÷ 9 =	63 ÷ 9 =

Time: _____   Score: _____

36 ÷ 9 =	18 ÷ 9 =	54 ÷ 9 =	0 ÷ 9 =
27 ÷ 9 =	9 ÷ 9 =	90 ÷ 9 =	63 ÷ 9 =
72 ÷ 9 =	36 ÷ 9 =	90 ÷ 9 =	0 ÷ 9 =
9 ÷ 9 =	63 ÷ 9 =	90 ÷ 9 =	0 ÷ 9 =
72 ÷ 9 =	63 ÷ 9 =	9 ÷ 9 =	0 ÷ 9 =
27 ÷ 9 =	63 ÷ 9 =	81 ÷ 9 =	45 ÷ 9 =
27 ÷ 9 =	0 ÷ 9 =	63 ÷ 9 =	18 ÷ 9 =
45 ÷ 9 =	72 ÷ 9 =	9 ÷ 9 =	27 ÷ 9 =
9 ÷ 9 =	45 ÷ 9 =	0 ÷ 9 =	18 ÷ 9 =
72 ÷ 9 =	27 ÷ 9 =	81 ÷ 9 =	36 ÷ 9 =
36 ÷ 9 =	72 ÷ 9 =	0 ÷ 9 =	9 ÷ 9 =
81 ÷ 9 =	27 ÷ 9 =	18 ÷ 9 =	90 ÷ 9 =
90 ÷ 9 =	45 ÷ 9 =	63 ÷ 9 =	18 ÷ 9 =
45 ÷ 9 =	9 ÷ 9 =	63 ÷ 9 =	81 ÷ 9 =
90 ÷ 9 =	27 ÷ 9 =	90 ÷ 9 =	45 ÷ 9 =
18 ÷ 9 =	9 ÷ 9 =	81 ÷ 9 =	45 ÷ 9 =
72 ÷ 9 =	18 ÷ 9 =	81 ÷ 9 =	18 ÷ 9 =
81 ÷ 9 =	72 ÷ 9 =	18 ÷ 9 =	9 ÷ 9 =

Time: _____   Score: _____

$0 \div 9 =$	$90 \div 9 =$	$18 \div 9 =$	$9 \div 9 =$
$54 \div 9 =$	$63 \div 9 =$	$54 \div 9 =$	$27 \div 9 =$
$0 \div 9 =$	$9 \div 9 =$	$63 \div 9 =$	$90 \div 9 =$
$54 \div 9 =$	$18 \div 9 =$	$27 \div 9 =$	$36 \div 9 =$
$81 \div 9 =$	$27 \div 9 =$	$72 \div 9 =$	$63 \div 9 =$
$36 \div 9 =$	$54 \div 9 =$	$72 \div 9 =$	$63 \div 9 =$
$63 \div 9 =$	$45 \div 9 =$	$54 \div 9 =$	$90 \div 9 =$
$18 \div 9 =$	$90 \div 9 =$	$36 \div 9 =$	$90 \div 9 =$
$36 \div 9 =$	$27 \div 9 =$	$9 \div 9 =$	$27 \div 9 =$
$9 \div 9 =$	$0 \div 9 =$	$63 \div 9 =$	$18 \div 9 =$
$81 \div 9 =$	$45 \div 9 =$	$72 \div 9 =$	$0 \div 9 =$
$45 \div 9 =$	$18 \div 9 =$	$45 \div 9 =$	$81 \div 9 =$
$36 \div 9 =$	$18 \div 9 =$	$27 \div 9 =$	$18 \div 9 =$
$54 \div 9 =$	$63 \div 9 =$	$54 \div 9 =$	$81 \div 9 =$
$90 \div 9 =$	$63 \div 9 =$	$36 \div 9 =$	$18 \div 9 =$
$9 \div 9 =$	$81 \div 9 =$	$36 \div 9 =$	$18 \div 9 =$
$72 \div 9 =$	$63 \div 9 =$	$90 \div 9 =$	$9 \div 9 =$
$18 \div 9 =$	$27 \div 9 =$	$72 \div 9 =$	$18 \div 9 =$

Time: _____   Score: _____

18 ÷ 9 =	72 ÷ 9 =	54 ÷ 9 =	90 ÷ 9 =
81 ÷ 9 =	63 ÷ 9 =	90 ÷ 9 =	27 ÷ 9 =
0 ÷ 9 =	63 ÷ 9 =	9 ÷ 9 =	27 ÷ 9 =
72 ÷ 9 =	9 ÷ 9 =	54 ÷ 9 =	81 ÷ 9 =
9 ÷ 9 =	45 ÷ 9 =	90 ÷ 9 =	54 ÷ 9 =
63 ÷ 9 =	54 ÷ 9 =	18 ÷ 9 =	63 ÷ 9 =
54 ÷ 9 =	81 ÷ 9 =	90 ÷ 9 =	72 ÷ 9 =
27 ÷ 9 =	0 ÷ 9 =	72 ÷ 9 =	45 ÷ 9 =
63 ÷ 9 =	36 ÷ 9 =	54 ÷ 9 =	27 ÷ 9 =
54 ÷ 9 =	63 ÷ 9 =	72 ÷ 9 =	27 ÷ 9 =
45 ÷ 9 =	72 ÷ 9 =	54 ÷ 9 =	0 ÷ 9 =
90 ÷ 9 =	0 ÷ 9 =	72 ÷ 9 =	81 ÷ 9 =
54 ÷ 9 =	18 ÷ 9 =	54 ÷ 9 =	90 ÷ 9 =
54 ÷ 9 =	9 ÷ 9 =	18 ÷ 9 =	45 ÷ 9 =
54 ÷ 9 =	0 ÷ 9 =	18 ÷ 9 =	36 ÷ 9 =
9 ÷ 9 =	54 ÷ 9 =	90 ÷ 9 =	45 ÷ 9 =
45 ÷ 9 =	27 ÷ 9 =	0 ÷ 9 =	63 ÷ 9 =
27 ÷ 9 =	18 ÷ 9 =	45 ÷ 9 =	9 ÷ 9 =

Time: _____   Score: _____

90 ÷ 10 =	0 ÷ 10 =	90 ÷ 10 =	80 ÷ 10 =
30 ÷ 10 =	60 ÷ 10 =	100 ÷ 10 =	50 ÷ 10 =
50 ÷ 10 =	30 ÷ 10 =	100 ÷ 10 =	50 ÷ 10 =
60 ÷ 10 =	10 ÷ 10 =	0 ÷ 10 =	10 ÷ 10 =
10 ÷ 10 =	40 ÷ 10 =	60 ÷ 10 =	100 ÷ 10 =
10 ÷ 10 =	50 ÷ 10 =	100 ÷ 10 =	20 ÷ 10 =
80 ÷ 10 =	50 ÷ 10 =	10 ÷ 10 =	100 ÷ 10 =
0 ÷ 10 =	50 ÷ 10 =	60 ÷ 10 =	50 ÷ 10 =
90 ÷ 10 =	20 ÷ 10 =	90 ÷ 10 =	100 ÷ 10 =
0 ÷ 10 =	90 ÷ 10 =	0 ÷ 10 =	20 ÷ 10 =
60 ÷ 10 =	100 ÷ 10 =	30 ÷ 10 =	90 ÷ 10 =
70 ÷ 10 =	30 ÷ 10 =	60 ÷ 10 =	10 ÷ 10 =
90 ÷ 10 =	50 ÷ 10 =	30 ÷ 10 =	90 ÷ 10 =
40 ÷ 10 =	20 ÷ 10 =	40 ÷ 10 =	90 ÷ 10 =
0 ÷ 10 =	60 ÷ 10 =	70 ÷ 10 =	100 ÷ 10 =
40 ÷ 10 =	90 ÷ 10 =	60 ÷ 10 =	10 ÷ 10 =
90 ÷ 10 =	10 ÷ 10 =	30 ÷ 10 =	100 ÷ 10 =
80 ÷ 10 =	100 ÷ 10 =	60 ÷ 10 =	100 ÷ 10 =

Time: _____   Score: _____

60 ÷ 10 =	10 ÷ 10 =	60 ÷ 10 =	80 ÷ 10 =
50 ÷ 10 =	40 ÷ 10 =	30 ÷ 10 =	0 ÷ 10 =
0 ÷ 10 =	60 ÷ 10 =	20 ÷ 10 =	0 ÷ 10 =
60 ÷ 10 =	30 ÷ 10 =	90 ÷ 10 =	70 ÷ 10 =
10 ÷ 10 =	100 ÷ 10 =	30 ÷ 10 =	90 ÷ 10 =
30 ÷ 10 =	50 ÷ 10 =	40 ÷ 10 =	80 ÷ 10 =
80 ÷ 10 =	100 ÷ 10 =	20 ÷ 10 =	80 ÷ 10 =
70 ÷ 10 =	10 ÷ 10 =	0 ÷ 10 =	70 ÷ 10 =
90 ÷ 10 =	70 ÷ 10 =	30 ÷ 10 =	60 ÷ 10 =
100 ÷ 10 =	60 ÷ 10 =	100 ÷ 10 =	0 ÷ 10 =
20 ÷ 10 =	70 ÷ 10 =	30 ÷ 10 =	90 ÷ 10 =
50 ÷ 10 =	10 ÷ 10 =	100 ÷ 10 =	90 ÷ 10 =
60 ÷ 10 =	10 ÷ 10 =	50 ÷ 10 =	10 ÷ 10 =
90 ÷ 10 =	80 ÷ 10 =	0 ÷ 10 =	70 ÷ 10 =
60 ÷ 10 =	10 ÷ 10 =	100 ÷ 10 =	70 ÷ 10 =
0 ÷ 10 =	30 ÷ 10 =	80 ÷ 10 =	100 ÷ 10 =
40 ÷ 10 =	30 ÷ 10 =	60 ÷ 10 =	40 ÷ 10 =
90 ÷ 10 =	40 ÷ 10 =	100 ÷ 10 =	90 ÷ 10 =

Time: _____   Score: _____

$60 \div 10 =$	$0 \div 10 =$	$30 \div 10 =$	$40 \div 10 =$
$70 \div 10 =$	$60 \div 10 =$	$40 \div 10 =$	$70 \div 10 =$
$60 \div 10 =$	$50 \div 10 =$	$20 \div 10 =$	$10 \div 10 =$
$50 \div 10 =$	$20 \div 10 =$	$100 \div 10 =$	$0 \div 10 =$
$70 \div 10 =$	$80 \div 10 =$	$0 \div 10 =$	$60 \div 10 =$
$90 \div 10 =$	$60 \div 10 =$	$20 \div 10 =$	$80 \div 10 =$
$90 \div 10 =$	$20 \div 10 =$	$40 \div 10 =$	$70 \div 10 =$
$0 \div 10 =$	$20 \div 10 =$	$0 \div 10 =$	$70 \div 10 =$
$20 \div 10 =$	$30 \div 10 =$	$70 \div 10 =$	$50 \div 10 =$
$30 \div 10 =$	$80 \div 10 =$	$0 \div 10 =$	$10 \div 10 =$
$80 \div 10 =$	$50 \div 10 =$	$30 \div 10 =$	$70 \div 10 =$
$90 \div 10 =$	$70 \div 10 =$	$30 \div 10 =$	$40 \div 10 =$
$10 \div 10 =$	$70 \div 10 =$	$90 \div 10 =$	$10 \div 10 =$
$90 \div 10 =$	$20 \div 10 =$	$100 \div 10 =$	$30 \div 10 =$
$100 \div 10 =$	$50 \div 10 =$	$90 \div 10 =$	$40 \div 10 =$
$70 \div 10 =$	$100 \div 10 =$	$10 \div 10 =$	$50 \div 10 =$
$80 \div 10 =$	$50 \div 10 =$	$70 \div 10 =$	$30 \div 10 =$
$90 \div 10 =$	$100 \div 10 =$	$40 \div 10 =$	$20 \div 10 =$

Time: _____   Score: _____

30 ÷ 10 =	40 ÷ 10 =	100 ÷ 10 =	30 ÷ 10 =
0 ÷ 10 =	80 ÷ 10 =	90 ÷ 10 =	80 ÷ 10 =
50 ÷ 10 =	40 ÷ 10 =	80 ÷ 10 =	0 ÷ 10 =
50 ÷ 10 =	70 ÷ 10 =	10 ÷ 10 =	50 ÷ 10 =
80 ÷ 10 =	30 ÷ 10 =	50 ÷ 10 =	60 ÷ 10 =
30 ÷ 10 =	60 ÷ 10 =	0 ÷ 10 =	10 ÷ 10 =
70 ÷ 10 =	50 ÷ 10 =	70 ÷ 10 =	50 ÷ 10 =
20 ÷ 10 =	70 ÷ 10 =	10 ÷ 10 =	100 ÷ 10 =
70 ÷ 10 =	30 ÷ 10 =	50 ÷ 10 =	100 ÷ 10 =
30 ÷ 10 =	40 ÷ 10 =	50 ÷ 10 =	20 ÷ 10 =
20 ÷ 10 =	80 ÷ 10 =	60 ÷ 10 =	10 ÷ 10 =
90 ÷ 10 =	0 ÷ 10 =	90 ÷ 10 =	10 ÷ 10 =
40 ÷ 10 =	100 ÷ 10 =	50 ÷ 10 =	90 ÷ 10 =
60 ÷ 10 =	80 ÷ 10 =	0 ÷ 10 =	60 ÷ 10 =
50 ÷ 10 =	80 ÷ 10 =	90 ÷ 10 =	50 ÷ 10 =
100 ÷ 10 =	20 ÷ 10 =	50 ÷ 10 =	90 ÷ 10 =
10 ÷ 10 =	30 ÷ 10 =	90 ÷ 10 =	70 ÷ 10 =
10 ÷ 10 =	40 ÷ 10 =	0 ÷ 10 =	80 ÷ 10 =

Part 2: Practice Mixed Division Facts up to Five

Time: _____   Score: _____

$0 \div 2 =$	$20 \div 2 =$	$0 \div 5 =$	$5 \div 5 =$
$16 \div 2 =$	$16 \div 4 =$	$8 \div 4 =$	$9 \div 3 =$
$8 \div 2 =$	$20 \div 4 =$	$32 \div 4 =$	$20 \div 2 =$
$15 \div 5 =$	$25 \div 5 =$	$32 \div 4 =$	$32 \div 4 =$
$40 \div 5 =$	$12 \div 2 =$	$35 \div 5 =$	$24 \div 3 =$
$40 \div 4 =$	$16 \div 2 =$	$8 \div 2 =$	$25 \div 5 =$
$0 \div 5 =$	$4 \div 1 =$	$18 \div 2 =$	$16 \div 4 =$
$0 \div 1 =$	$15 \div 3 =$	$30 \div 3 =$	$5 \div 1 =$
$10 \div 5 =$	$10 \div 2 =$	$9 \div 1 =$	$2 \div 1 =$
$25 \div 5 =$	$20 \div 5 =$	$9 \div 3 =$	$4 \div 1 =$
$12 \div 4 =$	$10 \div 1 =$	$2 \div 1 =$	$10 \div 1 =$
$4 \div 1 =$	$50 \div 5 =$	$0 \div 3 =$	$28 \div 4 =$
$12 \div 4 =$	$12 \div 2 =$	$28 \div 4 =$	$1 \div 1 =$
$18 \div 3 =$	$36 \div 4 =$	$12 \div 4 =$	$36 \div 4 =$
$9 \div 3 =$	$32 \div 4 =$	$12 \div 4 =$	$25 \div 5 =$
$0 \div 1 =$	$27 \div 3 =$	$6 \div 3 =$	$36 \div 4 =$
$16 \div 4 =$	$40 \div 5 =$	$40 \div 5 =$	$14 \div 2 =$

Time: _____   Score: _____

8 ÷ 4 =	8 ÷ 1 =	14 ÷ 2 =	45 ÷ 5 =
12 ÷ 3 =	0 ÷ 3 =	0 ÷ 2 =	20 ÷ 5 =
3 ÷ 1 =	14 ÷ 2 =	15 ÷ 3 =	8 ÷ 1 =
36 ÷ 4 =	18 ÷ 2 =	8 ÷ 2 =	35 ÷ 5 =
40 ÷ 5 =	50 ÷ 5 =	10 ÷ 1 =	6 ÷ 3 =
24 ÷ 3 =	8 ÷ 4 =	18 ÷ 2 =	2 ÷ 2 =
0 ÷ 5 =	3 ÷ 3 =	12 ÷ 3 =	2 ÷ 2 =
45 ÷ 5 =	25 ÷ 5 =	27 ÷ 3 =	6 ÷ 2 =
1 ÷ 1 =	10 ÷ 1 =	45 ÷ 5 =	40 ÷ 5 =
35 ÷ 5 =	3 ÷ 3 =	6 ÷ 2 =	1 ÷ 1 =
4 ÷ 4 =	35 ÷ 5 =	40 ÷ 4 =	30 ÷ 3 =
28 ÷ 4 =	45 ÷ 5 =	8 ÷ 1 =	9 ÷ 1 =
25 ÷ 5 =	28 ÷ 4 =	25 ÷ 5 =	10 ÷ 1 =
0 ÷ 3 =	2 ÷ 2 =	0 ÷ 4 =	15 ÷ 3 =
0 ÷ 4 =	12 ÷ 3 =	4 ÷ 1 =	27 ÷ 3 =
3 ÷ 1 =	20 ÷ 5 =	24 ÷ 4 =	18 ÷ 3 =
8 ÷ 2 =	20 ÷ 4 =	8 ÷ 4 =	9 ÷ 3 =
10 ÷ 5 =	8 ÷ 1 =	30 ÷ 5 =	4 ÷ 2 =

Time: _____   Score: _____

$50 \div 5 =$	$50 \div 5 =$	$10 \div 1 =$	$16 \div 4 =$
$35 \div 5 =$	$8 \div 4 =$	$12 \div 2 =$	$10 \div 1 =$
$14 \div 2 =$	$15 \div 5 =$	$45 \div 5 =$	$18 \div 2 =$
$18 \div 3 =$	$45 \div 5 =$	$24 \div 4 =$	$0 \div 1 =$
$24 \div 3 =$	$32 \div 4 =$	$1 \div 1 =$	$10 \div 1 =$
$0 \div 3 =$	$40 \div 5 =$	$7 \div 1 =$	$30 \div 5 =$
$35 \div 5 =$	$4 \div 4 =$	$6 \div 2 =$	$8 \div 1 =$
$45 \div 5 =$	$18 \div 2 =$	$32 \div 4 =$	$16 \div 2 =$
$6 \div 2 =$	$6 \div 2 =$	$14 \div 2 =$	$21 \div 3 =$
$16 \div 2 =$	$2 \div 1 =$	$9 \div 1 =$	$0 \div 5 =$
$2 \div 1 =$	$9 \div 3 =$	$6 \div 1 =$	$10 \div 5 =$
$20 \div 4 =$	$5 \div 5 =$	$14 \div 2 =$	$20 \div 2 =$
$24 \div 4 =$	$24 \div 4 =$	$24 \div 3 =$	$40 \div 5 =$
$6 \div 3 =$	$15 \div 5 =$	$30 \div 5 =$	$2 \div 2 =$
$3 \div 3 =$	$21 \div 3 =$	$18 \div 2 =$	$4 \div 4 =$
$16 \div 4 =$	$0 \div 5 =$	$30 \div 3 =$	$8 \div 2 =$
$25 \div 5 =$	$9 \div 1 =$	$12 \div 2 =$	$27 \div 3 =$
$6 \div 1 =$	$8 \div 1 =$	$30 \div 3 =$	$40 \div 5 =$

Time: _____   Score: _____

3 ÷ 1 =	14 ÷ 2 =	10 ÷ 5 =	35 ÷ 5 =
20 ÷ 5 =	27 ÷ 3 =	21 ÷ 3 =	21 ÷ 3 =
12 ÷ 2 =	7 ÷ 1 =	8 ÷ 4 =	18 ÷ 3 =
0 ÷ 5 =	4 ÷ 1 =	0 ÷ 5 =	3 ÷ 1 =
10 ÷ 1 =	15 ÷ 3 =	2 ÷ 1 =	28 ÷ 4 =
18 ÷ 3 =	0 ÷ 1 =	0 ÷ 3 =	20 ÷ 4 =
12 ÷ 3 =	0 ÷ 4 =	45 ÷ 5 =	4 ÷ 4 =
20 ÷ 5 =	8 ÷ 1 =	0 ÷ 3 =	18 ÷ 3 =
35 ÷ 5 =	4 ÷ 4 =	4 ÷ 1 =	18 ÷ 2 =
0 ÷ 4 =	15 ÷ 5 =	4 ÷ 4 =	6 ÷ 2 =
21 ÷ 3 =	18 ÷ 2 =	35 ÷ 5 =	50 ÷ 5 =
16 ÷ 4 =	24 ÷ 3 =	12 ÷ 3 =	30 ÷ 5 =
24 ÷ 3 =	4 ÷ 4 =	12 ÷ 4 =	2 ÷ 1 =
24 ÷ 3 =	30 ÷ 3 =	32 ÷ 4 =	3 ÷ 1 =
36 ÷ 4 =	50 ÷ 5 =	5 ÷ 1 =	10 ÷ 1 =
28 ÷ 4 =	0 ÷ 4 =	8 ÷ 2 =	1 ÷ 1 =
7 ÷ 1 =	16 ÷ 4 =	1 ÷ 1 =	0 ÷ 5 =
10 ÷ 5 =	24 ÷ 4 =	0 ÷ 2 =	10 ÷ 5 =

Time: _____   Score: _____

$14 \div 2 =$	$12 \div 2 =$	$5 \div 1 =$	$4 \div 2 =$
$6 \div 1 =$	$6 \div 2 =$	$18 \div 2 =$	$8 \div 1 =$
$20 \div 4 =$	$5 \div 5 =$	$20 \div 4 =$	$6 \div 2 =$
$0 \div 2 =$	$10 \div 2 =$	$40 \div 5 =$	$27 \div 3 =$
$40 \div 5 =$	$18 \div 2 =$	$0 \div 4 =$	$3 \div 3 =$
$8 \div 4 =$	$28 \div 4 =$	$32 \div 4 =$	$20 \div 4 =$
$6 \div 3 =$	$0 \div 1 =$	$30 \div 5 =$	$6 \div 1 =$
$20 \div 5 =$	$5 \div 1 =$	$25 \div 5 =$	$0 \div 5 =$
$3 \div 1 =$	$15 \div 3 =$	$24 \div 4 =$	$0 \div 3 =$
$15 \div 5 =$	$0 \div 3 =$	$20 \div 5 =$	$15 \div 3 =$
$16 \div 4 =$	$3 \div 1 =$	$20 \div 4 =$	$3 \div 3 =$
$16 \div 4 =$	$7 \div 1 =$	$21 \div 3 =$	$1 \div 1 =$
$4 \div 1 =$	$12 \div 4 =$	$12 \div 3 =$	$24 \div 3 =$
$20 \div 5 =$	$5 \div 5 =$	$36 \div 4 =$	$32 \div 4 =$
$5 \div 5 =$	$24 \div 4 =$	$3 \div 1 =$	$40 \div 5 =$
$8 \div 1 =$	$30 \div 3 =$	$15 \div 5 =$	$10 \div 2 =$
$20 \div 4 =$	$6 \div 2 =$	$10 \div 1 =$	$10 \div 2 =$
$0 \div 1 =$	$9 \div 3 =$	$16 \div 4 =$	$8 \div 4 =$

Time: _____   Score: _____

$7 \div 1 =$	$50 \div 5 =$	$6 \div 2 =$	$30 \div 3 =$
$2 \div 2 =$	$6 \div 2 =$	$15 \div 3 =$	$20 \div 2 =$
$18 \div 3 =$	$20 \div 2 =$	$3 \div 1 =$	$6 \div 2 =$
$10 \div 5 =$	$25 \div 5 =$	$14 \div 2 =$	$24 \div 4 =$
$6 \div 3 =$	$10 \div 1 =$	$36 \div 4 =$	$18 \div 3 =$
$2 \div 2 =$	$6 \div 2 =$	$3 \div 1 =$	$0 \div 1 =$
$20 \div 2 =$	$4 \div 4 =$	$30 \div 5 =$	$27 \div 3 =$
$0 \div 2 =$	$6 \div 2 =$	$16 \div 4 =$	$12 \div 2 =$
$10 \div 5 =$	$16 \div 2 =$	$36 \div 4 =$	$0 \div 1 =$
$15 \div 5 =$	$2 \div 2 =$	$2 \div 2 =$	$20 \div 2 =$
$4 \div 2 =$	$35 \div 5 =$	$1 \div 1 =$	$10 \div 5 =$
$10 \div 1 =$	$0 \div 1 =$	$18 \div 2 =$	$3 \div 1 =$
$15 \div 5 =$	$50 \div 5 =$	$15 \div 5 =$	$24 \div 4 =$
$12 \div 3 =$	$14 \div 2 =$	$5 \div 1 =$	$10 \div 2 =$
$32 \div 4 =$	$1 \div 1 =$	$0 \div 3 =$	$20 \div 2 =$
$28 \div 4 =$	$21 \div 3 =$	$45 \div 5 =$	$8 \div 1 =$
$2 \div 2 =$	$4 \div 4 =$	$24 \div 3 =$	$0 \div 5 =$
$1 \div 1 =$	$40 \div 5 =$	$0 \div 3 =$	$20 \div 4 =$

Time: _____   Score: _____

0 ÷ 5 =	35 ÷ 5 =	2 ÷ 1 =	5 ÷ 1 =
40 ÷ 5 =	0 ÷ 3 =	24 ÷ 3 =	24 ÷ 4 =
6 ÷ 1 =	3 ÷ 1 =	35 ÷ 5 =	6 ÷ 1 =
40 ÷ 5 =	32 ÷ 4 =	20 ÷ 5 =	24 ÷ 4 =
45 ÷ 5 =	25 ÷ 5 =	8 ÷ 4 =	16 ÷ 4 =
36 ÷ 4 =	20 ÷ 4 =	12 ÷ 2 =	18 ÷ 3 =
0 ÷ 3 =	2 ÷ 1 =	2 ÷ 2 =	7 ÷ 1 =
10 ÷ 1 =	45 ÷ 5 =	10 ÷ 5 =	9 ÷ 3 =
4 ÷ 1 =	0 ÷ 5 =	6 ÷ 2 =	0 ÷ 2 =
30 ÷ 3 =	8 ÷ 2 =	45 ÷ 5 =	9 ÷ 1 =
4 ÷ 2 =	12 ÷ 3 =	12 ÷ 2 =	8 ÷ 2 =
30 ÷ 5 =	20 ÷ 2 =	35 ÷ 5 =	4 ÷ 2 =
6 ÷ 3 =	20 ÷ 5 =	6 ÷ 1 =	40 ÷ 4 =
0 ÷ 1 =	12 ÷ 3 =	8 ÷ 2 =	3 ÷ 1 =
3 ÷ 3 =	5 ÷ 1 =	27 ÷ 3 =	21 ÷ 3 =
3 ÷ 1 =	6 ÷ 2 =	40 ÷ 5 =	14 ÷ 2 =
10 ÷ 2 =	6 ÷ 1 =	18 ÷ 3 =	35 ÷ 5 =
18 ÷ 2 =	0 ÷ 3 =	8 ÷ 4 =	45 ÷ 5 =

Time: _____   Score: _____

45 ÷ 5 =	24 ÷ 3 =	14 ÷ 2 =	45 ÷ 5 =
40 ÷ 5 =	40 ÷ 5 =	10 ÷ 2 =	24 ÷ 3 =
0 ÷ 2 =	0 ÷ 4 =	15 ÷ 3 =	12 ÷ 3 =
12 ÷ 3 =	28 ÷ 4 =	15 ÷ 3 =	45 ÷ 5 =
14 ÷ 2 =	45 ÷ 5 =	4 ÷ 2 =	28 ÷ 4 =
50 ÷ 5 =	12 ÷ 3 =	7 ÷ 1 =	8 ÷ 2 =
0 ÷ 4 =	8 ÷ 1 =	0 ÷ 1 =	45 ÷ 5 =
4 ÷ 2 =	6 ÷ 3 =	20 ÷ 5 =	12 ÷ 3 =
4 ÷ 4 =	6 ÷ 1 =	1 ÷ 1 =	1 ÷ 1 =
30 ÷ 3 =	35 ÷ 5 =	4 ÷ 2 =	4 ÷ 1 =
45 ÷ 5 =	8 ÷ 1 =	6 ÷ 1 =	5 ÷ 1 =
14 ÷ 2 =	0 ÷ 1 =	45 ÷ 5 =	0 ÷ 1 =
28 ÷ 4 =	30 ÷ 5 =	4 ÷ 2 =	10 ÷ 5 =
30 ÷ 3 =	10 ÷ 1 =	9 ÷ 3 =	24 ÷ 3 =
12 ÷ 2 =	24 ÷ 4 =	4 ÷ 2 =	3 ÷ 1 =
12 ÷ 3 =	8 ÷ 1 =	1 ÷ 1 =	40 ÷ 4 =
50 ÷ 5 =	10 ÷ 2 =	12 ÷ 2 =	15 ÷ 3 =
20 ÷ 2 =	50 ÷ 5 =	4 ÷ 1 =	50 ÷ 5 =

Time: _____   Score: _____

$4 \div 4 =$	$12 \div 4 =$	$28 \div 4 =$	$4 \div 1 =$
$0 \div 4 =$	$16 \div 4 =$	$4 \div 2 =$	$9 \div 3 =$
$40 \div 5 =$	$10 \div 5 =$	$21 \div 3 =$	$30 \div 3 =$
$4 \div 4 =$	$36 \div 4 =$	$12 \div 2 =$	$36 \div 4 =$
$12 \div 2 =$	$0 \div 4 =$	$36 \div 4 =$	$6 \div 3 =$
$12 \div 3 =$	$40 \div 5 =$	$27 \div 3 =$	$8 \div 1 =$
$4 \div 2 =$	$12 \div 4 =$	$32 \div 4 =$	$32 \div 4 =$
$35 \div 5 =$	$20 \div 4 =$	$7 \div 1 =$	$18 \div 3 =$
$20 \div 2 =$	$0 \div 4 =$	$9 \div 3 =$	$40 \div 4 =$
$4 \div 2 =$	$24 \div 3 =$	$2 \div 1 =$	$36 \div 4 =$
$4 \div 2 =$	$16 \div 4 =$	$10 \div 5 =$	$18 \div 2 =$
$20 \div 2 =$	$8 \div 1 =$	$21 \div 3 =$	$12 \div 3 =$
$6 \div 3 =$	$8 \div 4 =$	$18 \div 2 =$	$14 \div 2 =$
$8 \div 2 =$	$15 \div 5 =$	$16 \div 2 =$	$30 \div 5 =$
$12 \div 3 =$	$32 \div 4 =$	$9 \div 3 =$	$16 \div 2 =$
$10 \div 2 =$	$30 \div 3 =$	$40 \div 5 =$	$35 \div 5 =$
$32 \div 4 =$	$16 \div 2 =$	$27 \div 3 =$	$1 \div 1 =$
$30 \div 5 =$	$20 \div 2 =$	$1 \div 1 =$	$45 \div 5 =$

Time: _____   Score: _____

15 ÷ 3 =	5 ÷ 5 =	12 ÷ 4 =	6 ÷ 1 =
4 ÷ 2 =	18 ÷ 2 =	8 ÷ 4 =	20 ÷ 2 =
0 ÷ 2 =	2 ÷ 1 =	15 ÷ 5 =	4 ÷ 1 =
6 ÷ 3 =	18 ÷ 3 =	21 ÷ 3 =	6 ÷ 1 =
45 ÷ 5 =	15 ÷ 3 =	18 ÷ 3 =	10 ÷ 2 =
30 ÷ 5 =	15 ÷ 5 =	8 ÷ 4 =	15 ÷ 3 =
21 ÷ 3 =	10 ÷ 1 =	8 ÷ 4 =	28 ÷ 4 =
16 ÷ 4 =	10 ÷ 1 =	7 ÷ 1 =	6 ÷ 3 =
10 ÷ 1 =	0 ÷ 5 =	20 ÷ 5 =	8 ÷ 2 =
3 ÷ 1 =	20 ÷ 4 =	6 ÷ 2 =	24 ÷ 4 =
0 ÷ 2 =	6 ÷ 3 =	2 ÷ 1 =	4 ÷ 4 =
20 ÷ 5 =	8 ÷ 2 =	0 ÷ 2 =	30 ÷ 3 =
40 ÷ 5 =	20 ÷ 2 =	36 ÷ 4 =	30 ÷ 5 =
20 ÷ 2 =	20 ÷ 5 =	20 ÷ 5 =	45 ÷ 5 =
12 ÷ 4 =	15 ÷ 3 =	12 ÷ 3 =	12 ÷ 2 =
8 ÷ 2 =	35 ÷ 5 =	45 ÷ 5 =	50 ÷ 5 =
8 ÷ 2 =	40 ÷ 4 =	9 ÷ 1 =	6 ÷ 1 =
9 ÷ 3 =	18 ÷ 3 =	45 ÷ 5 =	12 ÷ 4 =

Time: _____   Score: _____

$10 \div 5 =$	$10 \div 5 =$	$0 \div 2 =$	$2 \div 1 =$
$0 \div 4 =$	$8 \div 2 =$	$4 \div 1 =$	$4 \div 2 =$
$50 \div 5 =$	$16 \div 2 =$	$0 \div 1 =$	$10 \div 5 =$
$0 \div 5 =$	$24 \div 3 =$	$6 \div 1 =$	$6 \div 2 =$
$18 \div 2 =$	$5 \div 1 =$	$6 \div 3 =$	$3 \div 1 =$
$1 \div 1 =$	$0 \div 1 =$	$16 \div 2 =$	$5 \div 1 =$
$12 \div 2 =$	$0 \div 4 =$	$4 \div 4 =$	$30 \div 3 =$
$15 \div 5 =$	$0 \div 5 =$	$10 \div 5 =$	$16 \div 2 =$
$6 \div 3 =$	$8 \div 2 =$	$6 \div 1 =$	$9 \div 1 =$
$6 \div 1 =$	$7 \div 1 =$	$4 \div 4 =$	$4 \div 1 =$
$35 \div 5 =$	$25 \div 5 =$	$9 \div 3 =$	$28 \div 4 =$
$12 \div 3 =$	$8 \div 1 =$	$20 \div 2 =$	$4 \div 1 =$
$40 \div 5 =$	$15 \div 5 =$	$30 \div 5 =$	$45 \div 5 =$
$12 \div 2 =$	$30 \div 5 =$	$0 \div 5 =$	$6 \div 1 =$
$3 \div 1 =$	$6 \div 1 =$	$36 \div 4 =$	$0 \div 5 =$
$20 \div 5 =$	$8 \div 4 =$	$2 \div 2 =$	$3 \div 1 =$
$8 \div 4 =$	$20 \div 2 =$	$40 \div 5 =$	$30 \div 5 =$
$0 \div 2 =$	$3 \div 1 =$	$12 \div 3 =$	$35 \div 5 =$

Time: _____   Score: _____

$5 \div 1 =$	$14 \div 2 =$	$24 \div 4 =$	$20 \div 4 =$
$30 \div 3 =$	$10 \div 5 =$	$4 \div 4 =$	$9 \div 1 =$
$30 \div 3 =$	$18 \div 3 =$	$4 \div 1 =$	$30 \div 3 =$
$0 \div 5 =$	$25 \div 5 =$	$0 \div 5 =$	$40 \div 4 =$
$27 \div 3 =$	$21 \div 3 =$	$8 \div 2 =$	$6 \div 3 =$
$24 \div 3 =$	$5 \div 1 =$	$21 \div 3 =$	$36 \div 4 =$
$20 \div 4 =$	$0 \div 2 =$	$3 \div 1 =$	$14 \div 2 =$
$20 \div 4 =$	$2 \div 1 =$	$20 \div 5 =$	$32 \div 4 =$
$21 \div 3 =$	$25 \div 5 =$	$28 \div 4 =$	$2 \div 1 =$
$30 \div 5 =$	$4 \div 4 =$	$12 \div 2 =$	$15 \div 5 =$
$30 \div 5 =$	$2 \div 1 =$	$1 \div 1 =$	$30 \div 3 =$
$10 \div 2 =$	$5 \div 5 =$	$18 \div 2 =$	$28 \div 4 =$
$24 \div 3 =$	$5 \div 5 =$	$4 \div 1 =$	$2 \div 1 =$
$4 \div 2 =$	$35 \div 5 =$	$4 \div 4 =$	$27 \div 3 =$
$2 \div 1 =$	$8 \div 2 =$	$12 \div 2 =$	$5 \div 5 =$
$9 \div 1 =$	$21 \div 3 =$	$12 \div 4 =$	$12 \div 3 =$
$7 \div 1 =$	$50 \div 5 =$	$4 \div 2 =$	$5 \div 5 =$
$35 \div 5 =$	$18 \div 3 =$	$15 \div 5 =$	$12 \div 4 =$

Time: _____   Score: _____

4 ÷ 4 =	35 ÷ 5 =	35 ÷ 5 =	2 ÷ 1 =
40 ÷ 4 =	4 ÷ 2 =	3 ÷ 1 =	20 ÷ 4 =
6 ÷ 1 =	35 ÷ 5 =	0 ÷ 5 =	15 ÷ 3 =
10 ÷ 1 =	21 ÷ 3 =	4 ÷ 4 =	12 ÷ 3 =
40 ÷ 5 =	25 ÷ 5 =	1 ÷ 1 =	0 ÷ 4 =
18 ÷ 2 =	5 ÷ 1 =	0 ÷ 2 =	4 ÷ 2 =
0 ÷ 3 =	2 ÷ 2 =	12 ÷ 4 =	35 ÷ 5 =
35 ÷ 5 =	36 ÷ 4 =	0 ÷ 4 =	0 ÷ 1 =
2 ÷ 2 =	27 ÷ 3 =	32 ÷ 4 =	14 ÷ 2 =
27 ÷ 3 =	20 ÷ 4 =	10 ÷ 1 =	5 ÷ 5 =
36 ÷ 4 =	8 ÷ 1 =	5 ÷ 5 =	0 ÷ 3 =
10 ÷ 1 =	4 ÷ 4 =	12 ÷ 3 =	24 ÷ 3 =
1 ÷ 1 =	6 ÷ 2 =	16 ÷ 4 =	4 ÷ 2 =
2 ÷ 1 =	24 ÷ 4 =	8 ÷ 1 =	8 ÷ 4 =
3 ÷ 1 =	15 ÷ 5 =	12 ÷ 2 =	18 ÷ 2 =
25 ÷ 5 =	12 ÷ 4 =	24 ÷ 3 =	14 ÷ 2 =
32 ÷ 4 =	10 ÷ 2 =	24 ÷ 3 =	6 ÷ 2 =
35 ÷ 5 =	30 ÷ 5 =	0 ÷ 4 =	20 ÷ 2 =

Time: _____   Score: _____

$3 \div 1 =$	$18 \div 2 =$	$12 \div 2 =$	$6 \div 1 =$
$0 \div 2 =$	$4 \div 2 =$	$3 \div 1 =$	$35 \div 5 =$
$30 \div 3 =$	$35 \div 5 =$	$4 \div 4 =$	$24 \div 3 =$
$35 \div 5 =$	$24 \div 4 =$	$40 \div 4 =$	$50 \div 5 =$
$30 \div 3 =$	$4 \div 2 =$	$12 \div 2 =$	$12 \div 2 =$
$6 \div 3 =$	$24 \div 3 =$	$2 \div 1 =$	$4 \div 1 =$
$4 \div 2 =$	$45 \div 5 =$	$32 \div 4 =$	$4 \div 4 =$
$0 \div 1 =$	$21 \div 3 =$	$24 \div 4 =$	$12 \div 2 =$
$35 \div 5 =$	$0 \div 5 =$	$2 \div 2 =$	$3 \div 3 =$
$18 \div 3 =$	$24 \div 3 =$	$14 \div 2 =$	$25 \div 5 =$
$36 \div 4 =$	$8 \div 4 =$	$50 \div 5 =$	$9 \div 3 =$
$2 \div 1 =$	$3 \div 1 =$	$0 \div 2 =$	$20 \div 5 =$
$40 \div 5 =$	$15 \div 3 =$	$8 \div 4 =$	$8 \div 1 =$
$2 \div 2 =$	$9 \div 1 =$	$1 \div 1 =$	$5 \div 1 =$
$15 \div 3 =$	$3 \div 3 =$	$10 \div 5 =$	$9 \div 1 =$
$9 \div 3 =$	$27 \div 3 =$	$3 \div 3 =$	$14 \div 2 =$
$30 \div 5 =$	$10 \div 1 =$	$9 \div 3 =$	$0 \div 3 =$
$35 \div 5 =$	$24 \div 3 =$	$6 \div 1 =$	$15 \div 3 =$

Time: _____   Score: _____

$20 \div 2 =$	$6 \div 1 =$	$21 \div 3 =$	$9 \div 3 =$
$12 \div 3 =$	$16 \div 4 =$	$6 \div 2 =$	$24 \div 4 =$
$24 \div 4 =$	$8 \div 4 =$	$30 \div 3 =$	$30 \div 3 =$
$20 \div 5 =$	$0 \div 3 =$	$24 \div 4 =$	$40 \div 5 =$
$9 \div 1 =$	$5 \div 1 =$	$6 \div 2 =$	$0 \div 2 =$
$9 \div 1 =$	$30 \div 3 =$	$12 \div 3 =$	$35 \div 5 =$
$25 \div 5 =$	$16 \div 2 =$	$4 \div 1 =$	$2 \div 2 =$
$9 \div 1 =$	$16 \div 2 =$	$10 \div 1 =$	$14 \div 2 =$
$27 \div 3 =$	$16 \div 4 =$	$16 \div 2 =$	$3 \div 1 =$
$12 \div 4 =$	$8 \div 2 =$	$10 \div 2 =$	$30 \div 3 =$
$3 \div 1 =$	$0 \div 3 =$	$18 \div 2 =$	$30 \div 5 =$
$6 \div 3 =$	$40 \div 5 =$	$15 \div 3 =$	$2 \div 2 =$
$25 \div 5 =$	$8 \div 1 =$	$16 \div 2 =$	$45 \div 5 =$
$16 \div 2 =$	$9 \div 3 =$	$27 \div 3 =$	$0 \div 2 =$
$20 \div 5 =$	$21 \div 3 =$	$30 \div 5 =$	$4 \div 2 =$
$50 \div 5 =$	$30 \div 3 =$	$3 \div 1 =$	$3 \div 1 =$
$4 \div 1 =$	$18 \div 3 =$	$14 \div 2 =$	$30 \div 5 =$
$9 \div 3 =$	$8 \div 4 =$	$8 \div 2 =$	$10 \div 1 =$

Time: _____   Score: _____

28 ÷ 4 =	8 ÷ 4 =	10 ÷ 2 =	16 ÷ 4 =
3 ÷ 1 =	28 ÷ 4 =	12 ÷ 2 =	30 ÷ 3 =
14 ÷ 2 =	12 ÷ 4 =	4 ÷ 4 =	8 ÷ 2 =
6 ÷ 3 =	0 ÷ 2 =	5 ÷ 5 =	28 ÷ 4 =
20 ÷ 5 =	4 ÷ 4 =	32 ÷ 4 =	12 ÷ 4 =
45 ÷ 5 =	10 ÷ 2 =	0 ÷ 4 =	2 ÷ 1 =
20 ÷ 4 =	8 ÷ 4 =	15 ÷ 5 =	8 ÷ 2 =
16 ÷ 4 =	5 ÷ 5 =	3 ÷ 1 =	50 ÷ 5 =
15 ÷ 3 =	7 ÷ 1 =	5 ÷ 1 =	35 ÷ 5 =
50 ÷ 5 =	15 ÷ 5 =	20 ÷ 2 =	5 ÷ 5 =
20 ÷ 4 =	10 ÷ 5 =	2 ÷ 1 =	36 ÷ 4 =
0 ÷ 5 =	24 ÷ 4 =	6 ÷ 1 =	0 ÷ 1 =
21 ÷ 3 =	21 ÷ 3 =	30 ÷ 3 =	4 ÷ 2 =
20 ÷ 5 =	12 ÷ 4 =	14 ÷ 2 =	18 ÷ 3 =
32 ÷ 4 =	14 ÷ 2 =	30 ÷ 5 =	10 ÷ 5 =
20 ÷ 5 =	8 ÷ 2 =	1 ÷ 1 =	7 ÷ 1 =
18 ÷ 2 =	5 ÷ 1 =	25 ÷ 5 =	4 ÷ 1 =
3 ÷ 1 =	24 ÷ 4 =	30 ÷ 5 =	40 ÷ 4 =

Time: _____   Score: _____

$4 \div 1 =$	$5 \div 5 =$	$4 \div 1 =$	$32 \div 4 =$
$4 \div 2 =$	$8 \div 1 =$	$2 \div 1 =$	$24 \div 3 =$
$50 \div 5 =$	$35 \div 5 =$	$12 \div 4 =$	$3 \div 3 =$
$10 \div 2 =$	$50 \div 5 =$	$24 \div 4 =$	$6 \div 1 =$
$21 \div 3 =$	$45 \div 5 =$	$40 \div 4 =$	$16 \div 2 =$
$28 \div 4 =$	$12 \div 3 =$	$9 \div 3 =$	$28 \div 4 =$
$9 \div 3 =$	$24 \div 3 =$	$0 \div 5 =$	$0 \div 4 =$
$27 \div 3 =$	$6 \div 3 =$	$30 \div 3 =$	$1 \div 1 =$
$15 \div 3 =$	$0 \div 1 =$	$30 \div 5 =$	$15 \div 3 =$
$7 \div 1 =$	$4 \div 2 =$	$5 \div 5 =$	$0 \div 5 =$
$16 \div 2 =$	$30 \div 5 =$	$15 \div 3 =$	$10 \div 2 =$
$30 \div 3 =$	$2 \div 2 =$	$30 \div 5 =$	$3 \div 3 =$
$10 \div 1 =$	$24 \div 3 =$	$5 \div 5 =$	$0 \div 2 =$
$12 \div 2 =$	$9 \div 1 =$	$45 \div 5 =$	$0 \div 5 =$
$0 \div 1 =$	$30 \div 5 =$	$15 \div 5 =$	$28 \div 4 =$
$9 \div 3 =$	$5 \div 5 =$	$15 \div 3 =$	$15 \div 5 =$
$4 \div 1 =$	$20 \div 5 =$	$0 \div 3 =$	$35 \div 5 =$
$20 \div 5 =$	$45 \div 5 =$	$6 \div 1 =$	$15 \div 5 =$

Time: _____   Score: _____

$40 \div 5 =$	$30 \div 5 =$	$24 \div 4 =$	$10 \div 2 =$
$0 \div 3 =$	$6 \div 1 =$	$36 \div 4 =$	$5 \div 5 =$
$3 \div 1 =$	$9 \div 1 =$	$10 \div 2 =$	$32 \div 4 =$
$10 \div 1 =$	$24 \div 3 =$	$0 \div 4 =$	$36 \div 4 =$
$9 \div 3 =$	$30 \div 3 =$	$8 \div 4 =$	$15 \div 5 =$
$50 \div 5 =$	$6 \div 1 =$	$36 \div 4 =$	$0 \div 4 =$
$40 \div 4 =$	$0 \div 1 =$	$40 \div 5 =$	$8 \div 2 =$
$9 \div 3 =$	$20 \div 5 =$	$20 \div 5 =$	$27 \div 3 =$
$0 \div 1 =$	$12 \div 3 =$	$18 \div 3 =$	$16 \div 4 =$
$18 \div 3 =$	$5 \div 1 =$	$28 \div 4 =$	$0 \div 3 =$
$27 \div 3 =$	$8 \div 4 =$	$9 \div 1 =$	$12 \div 3 =$
$0 \div 1 =$	$7 \div 1 =$	$12 \div 4 =$	$5 \div 1 =$
$4 \div 4 =$	$5 \div 1 =$	$35 \div 5 =$	$14 \div 2 =$
$35 \div 5 =$	$5 \div 5 =$	$10 \div 5 =$	$15 \div 5 =$
$25 \div 5 =$	$16 \div 4 =$	$20 \div 4 =$	$20 \div 4 =$
$15 \div 5 =$	$50 \div 5 =$	$8 \div 2 =$	$4 \div 2 =$
$20 \div 5 =$	$40 \div 5 =$	$36 \div 4 =$	$10 \div 2 =$
$20 \div 4 =$	$2 \div 2 =$	$8 \div 1 =$	$15 \div 3 =$

Time: _____   Score: _____

$18 \div 3 =$	$9 \div 3 =$	$3 \div 3 =$	$15 \div 3 =$
$5 \div 1 =$	$40 \div 4 =$	$6 \div 2 =$	$20 \div 2 =$
$8 \div 2 =$	$2 \div 1 =$	$24 \div 3 =$	$4 \div 4 =$
$0 \div 5 =$	$2 \div 2 =$	$20 \div 2 =$	$25 \div 5 =$
$24 \div 4 =$	$12 \div 2 =$	$40 \div 5 =$	$25 \div 5 =$
$4 \div 2 =$	$12 \div 4 =$	$27 \div 3 =$	$1 \div 1 =$
$32 \div 4 =$	$10 \div 2 =$	$36 \div 4 =$	$25 \div 5 =$
$18 \div 3 =$	$10 \div 2 =$	$40 \div 5 =$	$18 \div 3 =$
$4 \div 1 =$	$4 \div 4 =$	$21 \div 3 =$	$20 \div 5 =$
$14 \div 2 =$	$4 \div 4 =$	$35 \div 5 =$	$24 \div 3 =$
$10 \div 5 =$	$8 \div 4 =$	$5 \div 5 =$	$3 \div 1 =$
$6 \div 3 =$	$5 \div 1 =$	$21 \div 3 =$	$10 \div 5 =$
$10 \div 2 =$	$28 \div 4 =$	$30 \div 5 =$	$28 \div 4 =$
$2 \div 1 =$	$7 \div 1 =$	$10 \div 2 =$	$16 \div 4 =$
$10 \div 5 =$	$45 \div 5 =$	$18 \div 3 =$	$6 \div 2 =$
$8 \div 1 =$	$36 \div 4 =$	$24 \div 4 =$	$18 \div 2 =$
$7 \div 1 =$	$36 \div 4 =$	$14 \div 2 =$	$6 \div 3 =$
$15 \div 5 =$	$12 \div 4 =$	$7 \div 1 =$	$35 \div 5 =$

Time: _____   Score: _____

18 ÷ 2 =	0 ÷ 1 =	45 ÷ 5 =	45 ÷ 5 =
6 ÷ 3 =	12 ÷ 3 =	5 ÷ 5 =	36 ÷ 4 =
0 ÷ 2 =	8 ÷ 4 =	2 ÷ 2 =	30 ÷ 5 =
16 ÷ 4 =	40 ÷ 5 =	24 ÷ 3 =	27 ÷ 3 =
35 ÷ 5 =	18 ÷ 2 =	0 ÷ 5 =	20 ÷ 4 =
24 ÷ 4 =	32 ÷ 4 =	24 ÷ 3 =	15 ÷ 5 =
6 ÷ 3 =	8 ÷ 1 =	9 ÷ 3 =	21 ÷ 3 =
16 ÷ 4 =	12 ÷ 4 =	18 ÷ 3 =	15 ÷ 5 =
28 ÷ 4 =	35 ÷ 5 =	0 ÷ 3 =	12 ÷ 2 =
45 ÷ 5 =	10 ÷ 2 =	4 ÷ 2 =	6 ÷ 2 =
5 ÷ 1 =	35 ÷ 5 =	3 ÷ 1 =	1 ÷ 1 =
2 ÷ 1 =	14 ÷ 2 =	3 ÷ 1 =	21 ÷ 3 =
15 ÷ 3 =	8 ÷ 2 =	0 ÷ 3 =	10 ÷ 5 =
3 ÷ 3 =	21 ÷ 3 =	20 ÷ 5 =	16 ÷ 4 =
14 ÷ 2 =	10 ÷ 5 =	45 ÷ 5 =	5 ÷ 1 =
8 ÷ 2 =	20 ÷ 4 =	45 ÷ 5 =	9 ÷ 3 =
40 ÷ 4 =	9 ÷ 3 =	8 ÷ 2 =	24 ÷ 3 =
24 ÷ 3 =	40 ÷ 5 =	2 ÷ 1 =	27 ÷ 3 =

Time: _____   Score: _____

$18 \div 2 =$	$20 \div 2 =$	$45 \div 5 =$	$4 \div 4 =$
$9 \div 1 =$	$15 \div 5 =$	$4 \div 4 =$	$45 \div 5 =$
$15 \div 3 =$	$35 \div 5 =$	$0 \div 5 =$	$40 \div 5 =$
$10 \div 1 =$	$0 \div 5 =$	$50 \div 5 =$	$9 \div 1 =$
$4 \div 1 =$	$0 \div 4 =$	$18 \div 2 =$	$20 \div 5 =$
$30 \div 3 =$	$20 \div 2 =$	$36 \div 4 =$	$8 \div 2 =$
$12 \div 2 =$	$1 \div 1 =$	$2 \div 1 =$	$10 \div 2 =$
$15 \div 3 =$	$7 \div 1 =$	$15 \div 5 =$	$12 \div 2 =$
$30 \div 3 =$	$6 \div 1 =$	$10 \div 2 =$	$10 \div 5 =$
$40 \div 4 =$	$15 \div 5 =$	$0 \div 1 =$	$12 \div 4 =$
$20 \div 4 =$	$14 \div 2 =$	$7 \div 1 =$	$45 \div 5 =$
$14 \div 2 =$	$14 \div 2 =$	$25 \div 5 =$	$35 \div 5 =$
$0 \div 2 =$	$6 \div 3 =$	$0 \div 5 =$	$9 \div 3 =$
$16 \div 4 =$	$14 \div 2 =$	$8 \div 2 =$	$4 \div 2 =$
$15 \div 5 =$	$0 \div 2 =$	$28 \div 4 =$	$6 \div 1 =$
$21 \div 3 =$	$6 \div 2 =$	$0 \div 4 =$	$1 \div 1 =$
$4 \div 1 =$	$15 \div 3 =$	$40 \div 5 =$	$40 \div 5 =$
$8 \div 4 =$	$6 \div 1 =$	$21 \div 3 =$	$18 \div 2 =$

Time: _____   Score: _____

24 ÷ 4 =	3 ÷ 3 =	15 ÷ 3 =	9 ÷ 3 =
0 ÷ 4 =	0 ÷ 4 =	0 ÷ 2 =	30 ÷ 3 =
1 ÷ 1 =	20 ÷ 4 =	20 ÷ 4 =	0 ÷ 3 =
28 ÷ 4 =	15 ÷ 5 =	9 ÷ 3 =	1 ÷ 1 =
5 ÷ 5 =	10 ÷ 1 =	21 ÷ 3 =	9 ÷ 1 =
10 ÷ 2 =	28 ÷ 4 =	7 ÷ 1 =	40 ÷ 4 =
12 ÷ 3 =	40 ÷ 4 =	0 ÷ 5 =	0 ÷ 5 =
15 ÷ 5 =	2 ÷ 2 =	15 ÷ 5 =	50 ÷ 5 =
0 ÷ 1 =	30 ÷ 3 =	15 ÷ 3 =	6 ÷ 2 =
16 ÷ 2 =	18 ÷ 3 =	20 ÷ 5 =	10 ÷ 2 =
30 ÷ 3 =	8 ÷ 1 =	12 ÷ 3 =	28 ÷ 4 =
2 ÷ 1 =	2 ÷ 2 =	8 ÷ 1 =	8 ÷ 4 =
20 ÷ 5 =	6 ÷ 1 =	10 ÷ 2 =	25 ÷ 5 =
6 ÷ 3 =	14 ÷ 2 =	14 ÷ 2 =	8 ÷ 1 =
30 ÷ 5 =	16 ÷ 4 =	40 ÷ 4 =	10 ÷ 5 =
10 ÷ 5 =	28 ÷ 4 =	21 ÷ 3 =	18 ÷ 3 =
10 ÷ 2 =	7 ÷ 1 =	0 ÷ 4 =	2 ÷ 2 =
4 ÷ 2 =	0 ÷ 4 =	30 ÷ 3 =	16 ÷ 2 =

Time: _____   Score: _____

$12 \div 2 =$	$10 \div 1 =$	$40 \div 4 =$	$6 \div 3 =$
$18 \div 3 =$	$18 \div 2 =$	$8 \div 4 =$	$30 \div 5 =$
$0 \div 2 =$	$18 \div 3 =$	$9 \div 1 =$	$21 \div 3 =$
$1 \div 1 =$	$0 \div 3 =$	$36 \div 4 =$	$3 \div 1 =$
$35 \div 5 =$	$5 \div 5 =$	$21 \div 3 =$	$6 \div 1 =$
$12 \div 3 =$	$20 \div 4 =$	$4 \div 2 =$	$8 \div 1 =$
$0 \div 3 =$	$14 \div 2 =$	$30 \div 3 =$	$6 \div 3 =$
$1 \div 1 =$	$12 \div 4 =$	$21 \div 3 =$	$0 \div 2 =$
$24 \div 3 =$	$4 \div 4 =$	$5 \div 5 =$	$7 \div 1 =$
$30 \div 5 =$	$0 \div 4 =$	$1 \div 1 =$	$12 \div 4 =$
$12 \div 3 =$	$8 \div 4 =$	$50 \div 5 =$	$16 \div 2 =$
$12 \div 3 =$	$5 \div 5 =$	$1 \div 1 =$	$12 \div 2 =$
$14 \div 2 =$	$1 \div 1 =$	$30 \div 3 =$	$8 \div 4 =$
$6 \div 1 =$	$21 \div 3 =$	$0 \div 2 =$	$15 \div 3 =$
$27 \div 3 =$	$8 \div 4 =$	$18 \div 3 =$	$6 \div 1 =$
$0 \div 4 =$	$14 \div 2 =$	$25 \div 5 =$	$4 \div 4 =$
$8 \div 4 =$	$16 \div 2 =$	$6 \div 1 =$	$10 \div 2 =$
$20 \div 2 =$	$9 \div 1 =$	$0 \div 3 =$	$18 \div 2 =$

Time: _____   Score: _____

$40 \div 5 =$	$36 \div 4 =$	$0 \div 4 =$	$21 \div 3 =$
$50 \div 5 =$	$3 \div 3 =$	$20 \div 2 =$	$30 \div 5 =$
$50 \div 5 =$	$12 \div 3 =$	$40 \div 4 =$	$12 \div 4 =$
$9 \div 3 =$	$10 \div 2 =$	$6 \div 2 =$	$20 \div 4 =$
$0 \div 1 =$	$0 \div 3 =$	$2 \div 1 =$	$12 \div 4 =$
$20 \div 2 =$	$0 \div 3 =$	$5 \div 1 =$	$14 \div 2 =$
$4 \div 4 =$	$2 \div 1 =$	$7 \div 1 =$	$14 \div 2 =$
$4 \div 2 =$	$6 \div 1 =$	$2 \div 2 =$	$0 \div 2 =$
$0 \div 5 =$	$30 \div 5 =$	$0 \div 3 =$	$8 \div 4 =$
$30 \div 3 =$	$20 \div 4 =$	$12 \div 4 =$	$3 \div 3 =$
$40 \div 4 =$	$10 \div 1 =$	$24 \div 3 =$	$18 \div 3 =$
$1 \div 1 =$	$36 \div 4 =$	$0 \div 4 =$	$24 \div 4 =$
$6 \div 1 =$	$20 \div 5 =$	$0 \div 4 =$	$14 \div 2 =$
$10 \div 1 =$	$2 \div 1 =$	$1 \div 1 =$	$45 \div 5 =$
$15 \div 5 =$	$25 \div 5 =$	$0 \div 5 =$	$0 \div 1 =$
$8 \div 4 =$	$9 \div 3 =$	$0 \div 3 =$	$8 \div 4 =$
$24 \div 3 =$	$9 \div 3 =$	$5 \div 5 =$	$10 \div 1 =$
$8 \div 1 =$	$16 \div 4 =$	$20 \div 2 =$	$9 \div 1 =$

Time: _____   Score: _____

12 ÷ 3 =	15 ÷ 5 =	12 ÷ 4 =	14 ÷ 2 =
6 ÷ 3 =	24 ÷ 4 =	4 ÷ 4 =	8 ÷ 1 =
24 ÷ 3 =	36 ÷ 4 =	4 ÷ 4 =	10 ÷ 2 =
0 ÷ 4 =	18 ÷ 2 =	18 ÷ 3 =	36 ÷ 4 =
16 ÷ 2 =	4 ÷ 1 =	14 ÷ 2 =	1 ÷ 1 =
3 ÷ 1 =	24 ÷ 3 =	36 ÷ 4 =	9 ÷ 3 =
4 ÷ 1 =	45 ÷ 5 =	28 ÷ 4 =	24 ÷ 3 =
4 ÷ 2 =	24 ÷ 4 =	9 ÷ 3 =	6 ÷ 1 =
1 ÷ 1 =	50 ÷ 5 =	18 ÷ 2 =	30 ÷ 3 =
3 ÷ 3 =	16 ÷ 4 =	16 ÷ 2 =	0 ÷ 3 =
20 ÷ 4 =	5 ÷ 1 =	20 ÷ 2 =	30 ÷ 5 =
21 ÷ 3 =	2 ÷ 1 =	50 ÷ 5 =	20 ÷ 5 =
6 ÷ 2 =	4 ÷ 4 =	27 ÷ 3 =	32 ÷ 4 =
24 ÷ 4 =	0 ÷ 5 =	0 ÷ 1 =	27 ÷ 3 =
3 ÷ 3 =	2 ÷ 1 =	3 ÷ 3 =	20 ÷ 5 =
3 ÷ 1 =	30 ÷ 5 =	4 ÷ 1 =	18 ÷ 2 =
15 ÷ 5 =	45 ÷ 5 =	30 ÷ 3 =	16 ÷ 2 =
3 ÷ 3 =	32 ÷ 4 =	8 ÷ 4 =	6 ÷ 1 =

Part 3: Practice Mixed Division Facts above Five

Time: _____   Score: _____

0 ÷ 7 =	80 ÷ 8 =	0 ÷ 10 =	30 ÷ 6 =
12 ÷ 6 =	24 ÷ 6 =	10 ÷ 10 =	64 ÷ 8 =
60 ÷ 6 =	36 ÷ 9 =	6 ÷ 6 =	20 ÷ 10 =
0 ÷ 6 =	54 ÷ 6 =	27 ÷ 9 =	28 ÷ 7 =
45 ÷ 9 =	72 ÷ 9 =	70 ÷ 7 =	30 ÷ 10 =
50 ÷ 10 =	72 ÷ 9 =	72 ÷ 9 =	24 ÷ 6 =
80 ÷ 10 =	48 ÷ 8 =	70 ÷ 10 =	64 ÷ 8 =
90 ÷ 9 =	64 ÷ 8 =	28 ÷ 7 =	50 ÷ 10 =
0 ÷ 10 =	24 ÷ 6 =	63 ÷ 7 =	36 ÷ 9 =
0 ÷ 6 =	40 ÷ 8 =	18 ÷ 6 =	80 ÷ 8 =
30 ÷ 6 =	20 ÷ 10 =	35 ÷ 7 =	63 ÷ 7 =
42 ÷ 6 =	14 ÷ 7 =	50 ÷ 10 =	40 ÷ 10 =
24 ÷ 8 =	0 ÷ 6 =	28 ÷ 7 =	27 ÷ 9 =
70 ÷ 7 =	12 ÷ 6 =	70 ÷ 7 =	48 ÷ 6 =
24 ÷ 6 =	100 ÷ 10 =	0 ÷ 9 =	70 ÷ 10 =
27 ÷ 9 =	48 ÷ 8 =	60 ÷ 6 =	63 ÷ 9 =
0 ÷ 6 =	12 ÷ 6 =	7 ÷ 7 =	54 ÷ 9 =

Time: _____   Score: _____

24 ÷ 8 =	72 ÷ 9 =	6 ÷ 6 =	27 ÷ 9 =
50 ÷ 10 =	0 ÷ 7 =	81 ÷ 9 =	16 ÷ 8 =
81 ÷ 9 =	36 ÷ 9 =	80 ÷ 10 =	80 ÷ 10 =
49 ÷ 7 =	16 ÷ 8 =	70 ÷ 7 =	100 ÷ 10 =
42 ÷ 7 =	18 ÷ 9 =	48 ÷ 6 =	56 ÷ 8 =
90 ÷ 10 =	36 ÷ 9 =	0 ÷ 9 =	0 ÷ 6 =
12 ÷ 6 =	0 ÷ 7 =	42 ÷ 6 =	40 ÷ 10 =
12 ÷ 6 =	21 ÷ 7 =	56 ÷ 8 =	40 ÷ 8 =
56 ÷ 7 =	90 ÷ 10 =	72 ÷ 8 =	0 ÷ 6 =
28 ÷ 7 =	70 ÷ 10 =	80 ÷ 10 =	100 ÷ 10 =
70 ÷ 7 =	18 ÷ 9 =	72 ÷ 9 =	20 ÷ 10 =
63 ÷ 7 =	8 ÷ 8 =	0 ÷ 10 =	9 ÷ 9 =
36 ÷ 9 =	8 ÷ 8 =	90 ÷ 10 =	50 ÷ 10 =
72 ÷ 8 =	24 ÷ 8 =	7 ÷ 7 =	70 ÷ 7 =
90 ÷ 10 =	80 ÷ 10 =	70 ÷ 10 =	8 ÷ 8 =
21 ÷ 7 =	12 ÷ 6 =	6 ÷ 6 =	9 ÷ 9 =
70 ÷ 10 =	90 ÷ 9 =	90 ÷ 9 =	63 ÷ 9 =
90 ÷ 10 =	56 ÷ 7 =	63 ÷ 7 =	60 ÷ 6 =

Time: _____   Score: _____

50 ÷ 10 =	48 ÷ 6 =	63 ÷ 9 =	50 ÷ 10 =
6 ÷ 6 =	70 ÷ 7 =	0 ÷ 8 =	7 ÷ 7 =
18 ÷ 6 =	0 ÷ 9 =	60 ÷ 6 =	40 ÷ 8 =
0 ÷ 9 =	32 ÷ 8 =	24 ÷ 6 =	28 ÷ 7 =
72 ÷ 8 =	21 ÷ 7 =	40 ÷ 10 =	60 ÷ 10 =
24 ÷ 6 =	48 ÷ 8 =	28 ÷ 7 =	45 ÷ 9 =
18 ÷ 9 =	12 ÷ 6 =	27 ÷ 9 =	20 ÷ 10 =
56 ÷ 7 =	60 ÷ 10 =	16 ÷ 8 =	100 ÷ 10 =
100 ÷ 10 =	70 ÷ 7 =	36 ÷ 9 =	70 ÷ 10 =
18 ÷ 9 =	42 ÷ 7 =	70 ÷ 7 =	56 ÷ 8 =
30 ÷ 10 =	90 ÷ 10 =	72 ÷ 8 =	54 ÷ 9 =
0 ÷ 6 =	90 ÷ 10 =	54 ÷ 9 =	18 ÷ 6 =
0 ÷ 7 =	64 ÷ 8 =	72 ÷ 9 =	7 ÷ 7 =
70 ÷ 7 =	0 ÷ 9 =	80 ÷ 10 =	49 ÷ 7 =
60 ÷ 10 =	70 ÷ 10 =	9 ÷ 9 =	21 ÷ 7 =
56 ÷ 7 =	90 ÷ 10 =	72 ÷ 8 =	72 ÷ 9 =
56 ÷ 7 =	24 ÷ 8 =	24 ÷ 8 =	49 ÷ 7 =
6 ÷ 6 =	56 ÷ 8 =	64 ÷ 8 =	14 ÷ 7 =

Time: _____   Score: _____

$54 \div 6 =$	$0 \div 10 =$	$14 \div 7 =$	$27 \div 9 =$
$42 \div 7 =$	$20 \div 10 =$	$45 \div 9 =$	$10 \div 10 =$
$49 \div 7 =$	$80 \div 8 =$	$30 \div 6 =$	$60 \div 10 =$
$54 \div 9 =$	$72 \div 9 =$	$80 \div 10 =$	$16 \div 8 =$
$30 \div 10 =$	$0 \div 6 =$	$60 \div 10 =$	$8 \div 8 =$
$8 \div 8 =$	$56 \div 8 =$	$72 \div 8 =$	$10 \div 10 =$
$18 \div 6 =$	$36 \div 9 =$	$0 \div 6 =$	$42 \div 6 =$
$0 \div 10 =$	$90 \div 9 =$	$32 \div 8 =$	$50 \div 10 =$
$63 \div 7 =$	$42 \div 7 =$	$42 \div 6 =$	$72 \div 8 =$
$42 \div 7 =$	$60 \div 6 =$	$56 \div 7 =$	$80 \div 8 =$
$80 \div 10 =$	$21 \div 7 =$	$49 \div 7 =$	$20 \div 10 =$
$70 \div 10 =$	$40 \div 10 =$	$12 \div 6 =$	$12 \div 6 =$
$72 \div 8 =$	$48 \div 6 =$	$63 \div 9 =$	$56 \div 8 =$
$48 \div 8 =$	$49 \div 7 =$	$18 \div 9 =$	$54 \div 9 =$
$24 \div 6 =$	$0 \div 10 =$	$28 \div 7 =$	$0 \div 10 =$
$21 \div 7 =$	$70 \div 7 =$	$45 \div 9 =$	$54 \div 6 =$
$14 \div 7 =$	$63 \div 9 =$	$48 \div 8 =$	$0 \div 7 =$
$48 \div 6 =$	$48 \div 6 =$	$6 \div 6 =$	$6 \div 6 =$

Time: _____   Score: _____

$0 \div 8 =$	$45 \div 9 =$	$36 \div 9 =$	$6 \div 6 =$
$0 \div 9 =$	$90 \div 10 =$	$0 \div 6 =$	$9 \div 9 =$
$0 \div 6 =$	$40 \div 10 =$	$56 \div 7 =$	$0 \div 8 =$
$48 \div 8 =$	$70 \div 10 =$	$6 \div 6 =$	$9 \div 9 =$
$28 \div 7 =$	$63 \div 7 =$	$12 \div 6 =$	$0 \div 9 =$
$30 \div 10 =$	$48 \div 6 =$	$48 \div 6 =$	$10 \div 10 =$
$24 \div 8 =$	$63 \div 9 =$	$63 \div 7 =$	$70 \div 10 =$
$100 \div 10 =$	$36 \div 9 =$	$18 \div 6 =$	$0 \div 6 =$
$64 \div 8 =$	$32 \div 8 =$	$12 \div 6 =$	$60 \div 10 =$
$64 \div 8 =$	$10 \div 10 =$	$27 \div 9 =$	$12 \div 6 =$
$72 \div 9 =$	$80 \div 8 =$	$72 \div 9 =$	$18 \div 6 =$
$90 \div 10 =$	$100 \div 10 =$	$30 \div 6 =$	$70 \div 7 =$
$63 \div 9 =$	$0 \div 9 =$	$32 \div 8 =$	$7 \div 7 =$
$49 \div 7 =$	$40 \div 10 =$	$7 \div 7 =$	$0 \div 10 =$
$24 \div 6 =$	$20 \div 10 =$	$54 \div 9 =$	$0 \div 7 =$
$20 \div 10 =$	$49 \div 7 =$	$42 \div 7 =$	$35 \div 7 =$
$16 \div 8 =$	$36 \div 6 =$	$24 \div 8 =$	$72 \div 8 =$
$56 \div 7 =$	$45 \div 9 =$	$10 \div 10 =$	$45 \div 9 =$

Time: _____   Score: _____

$24 \div 8 =$	$54 \div 6 =$	$0 \div 8 =$	$60 \div 6 =$
$40 \div 8 =$	$80 \div 10 =$	$81 \div 9 =$	$80 \div 10 =$
$72 \div 8 =$	$0 \div 9 =$	$8 \div 8 =$	$24 \div 6 =$
$18 \div 9 =$	$63 \div 9 =$	$72 \div 9 =$	$45 \div 9 =$
$16 \div 8 =$	$0 \div 7 =$	$60 \div 10 =$	$42 \div 7 =$
$60 \div 6 =$	$40 \div 10 =$	$30 \div 6 =$	$50 \div 10 =$
$0 \div 10 =$	$60 \div 6 =$	$21 \div 7 =$	$45 \div 9 =$
$54 \div 9 =$	$0 \div 8 =$	$30 \div 10 =$	$0 \div 9 =$
$40 \div 10 =$	$40 \div 8 =$	$36 \div 9 =$	$21 \div 7 =$
$45 \div 9 =$	$9 \div 9 =$	$40 \div 10 =$	$49 \div 7 =$
$56 \div 8 =$	$0 \div 6 =$	$6 \div 6 =$	$24 \div 6 =$
$27 \div 9 =$	$32 \div 8 =$	$36 \div 6 =$	$64 \div 8 =$
$40 \div 10 =$	$10 \div 10 =$	$12 \div 6 =$	$81 \div 9 =$
$72 \div 9 =$	$10 \div 10 =$	$54 \div 9 =$	$42 \div 6 =$
$18 \div 6 =$	$80 \div 10 =$	$56 \div 7 =$	$80 \div 8 =$
$30 \div 10 =$	$35 \div 7 =$	$45 \div 9 =$	$24 \div 8 =$
$70 \div 7 =$	$40 \div 8 =$	$48 \div 6 =$	$0 \div 7 =$
$27 \div 9 =$	$40 \div 10 =$	$12 \div 6 =$	$0 \div 6 =$

Time: _____   Score: _____

18 ÷ 9 =	49 ÷ 7 =	100 ÷ 10 =	24 ÷ 6 =
18 ÷ 6 =	21 ÷ 7 =	80 ÷ 8 =	8 ÷ 8 =
48 ÷ 6 =	21 ÷ 7 =	45 ÷ 9 =	80 ÷ 8 =
36 ÷ 6 =	54 ÷ 9 =	80 ÷ 8 =	18 ÷ 6 =
24 ÷ 8 =	20 ÷ 10 =	50 ÷ 10 =	49 ÷ 7 =
54 ÷ 9 =	18 ÷ 9 =	60 ÷ 6 =	90 ÷ 10 =
48 ÷ 8 =	7 ÷ 7 =	24 ÷ 8 =	42 ÷ 6 =
18 ÷ 6 =	60 ÷ 6 =	0 ÷ 7 =	70 ÷ 7 =
42 ÷ 6 =	9 ÷ 9 =	60 ÷ 10 =	72 ÷ 8 =
48 ÷ 6 =	0 ÷ 8 =	24 ÷ 8 =	36 ÷ 9 =
42 ÷ 7 =	20 ÷ 10 =	64 ÷ 8 =	81 ÷ 9 =
30 ÷ 6 =	0 ÷ 7 =	30 ÷ 10 =	7 ÷ 7 =
7 ÷ 7 =	70 ÷ 7 =	16 ÷ 8 =	70 ÷ 10 =
7 ÷ 7 =	20 ÷ 10 =	70 ÷ 7 =	0 ÷ 7 =
0 ÷ 6 =	63 ÷ 7 =	48 ÷ 6 =	18 ÷ 6 =
60 ÷ 6 =	30 ÷ 10 =	100 ÷ 10 =	30 ÷ 10 =
30 ÷ 6 =	54 ÷ 9 =	32 ÷ 8 =	56 ÷ 8 =
35 ÷ 7 =	40 ÷ 8 =	6 ÷ 6 =	72 ÷ 9 =

Time: _____   Score: _____

12 ÷ 6 =	7 ÷ 7 =	36 ÷ 6 =	0 ÷ 6 =
0 ÷ 8 =	70 ÷ 7 =	63 ÷ 9 =	63 ÷ 9 =
90 ÷ 10 =	48 ÷ 6 =	7 ÷ 7 =	9 ÷ 9 =
64 ÷ 8 =	0 ÷ 10 =	7 ÷ 7 =	18 ÷ 6 =
80 ÷ 10 =	0 ÷ 9 =	45 ÷ 9 =	30 ÷ 6 =
42 ÷ 6 =	0 ÷ 10 =	42 ÷ 6 =	70 ÷ 10 =
14 ÷ 7 =	30 ÷ 6 =	18 ÷ 6 =	80 ÷ 10 =
0 ÷ 9 =	64 ÷ 8 =	60 ÷ 10 =	18 ÷ 6 =
36 ÷ 6 =	18 ÷ 6 =	70 ÷ 10 =	42 ÷ 7 =
80 ÷ 10 =	72 ÷ 9 =	40 ÷ 10 =	30 ÷ 6 =
54 ÷ 9 =	90 ÷ 10 =	18 ÷ 6 =	50 ÷ 10 =
18 ÷ 9 =	40 ÷ 10 =	90 ÷ 10 =	45 ÷ 9 =
42 ÷ 7 =	24 ÷ 6 =	18 ÷ 6 =	48 ÷ 8 =
0 ÷ 6 =	0 ÷ 9 =	14 ÷ 7 =	8 ÷ 8 =
49 ÷ 7 =	70 ÷ 7 =	90 ÷ 10 =	20 ÷ 10 =
27 ÷ 9 =	28 ÷ 7 =	0 ÷ 10 =	21 ÷ 7 =
0 ÷ 8 =	80 ÷ 8 =	32 ÷ 8 =	90 ÷ 10 =
63 ÷ 7 =	16 ÷ 8 =	32 ÷ 8 =	48 ÷ 8 =

Time: _____   Score: _____

$28 \div 7 =$	$60 \div 10 =$	$18 \div 6 =$	$70 \div 7 =$
$70 \div 10 =$	$30 \div 6 =$	$14 \div 7 =$	$16 \div 8 =$
$40 \div 10 =$	$36 \div 6 =$	$90 \div 9 =$	$0 \div 7 =$
$32 \div 8 =$	$32 \div 8 =$	$21 \div 7 =$	$8 \div 8 =$
$35 \div 7 =$	$81 \div 9 =$	$54 \div 6 =$	$63 \div 9 =$
$21 \div 7 =$	$24 \div 8 =$	$80 \div 10 =$	$49 \div 7 =$
$40 \div 8 =$	$42 \div 7 =$	$48 \div 8 =$	$70 \div 10 =$
$63 \div 7 =$	$0 \div 8 =$	$18 \div 9 =$	$90 \div 10 =$
$90 \div 10 =$	$72 \div 9 =$	$56 \div 8 =$	$90 \div 10 =$
$0 \div 6 =$	$42 \div 6 =$	$80 \div 10 =$	$80 \div 10 =$
$40 \div 8 =$	$0 \div 6 =$	$64 \div 8 =$	$12 \div 6 =$
$0 \div 7 =$	$0 \div 9 =$	$45 \div 9 =$	$36 \div 6 =$
$30 \div 6 =$	$32 \div 8 =$	$32 \div 8 =$	$63 \div 9 =$
$40 \div 8 =$	$90 \div 10 =$	$49 \div 7 =$	$90 \div 10 =$
$16 \div 8 =$	$70 \div 10 =$	$100 \div 10 =$	$48 \div 6 =$
$36 \div 9 =$	$49 \div 7 =$	$28 \div 7 =$	$0 \div 10 =$
$56 \div 7 =$	$0 \div 6 =$	$90 \div 10 =$	$16 \div 8 =$
$16 \div 8 =$	$0 \div 6 =$	$12 \div 6 =$	$24 \div 6 =$

Time: _____   Score: _____

$40 \div 10 =$	$36 \div 9 =$	$9 \div 9 =$	$36 \div 6 =$
$6 \div 6 =$	$36 \div 6 =$	$6 \div 6 =$	$80 \div 8 =$
$70 \div 10 =$	$16 \div 8 =$	$28 \div 7 =$	$90 \div 10 =$
$18 \div 6 =$	$48 \div 6 =$	$36 \div 6 =$	$35 \div 7 =$
$49 \div 7 =$	$0 \div 7 =$	$90 \div 10 =$	$0 \div 7 =$
$63 \div 9 =$	$60 \div 10 =$	$16 \div 8 =$	$20 \div 10 =$
$80 \div 8 =$	$70 \div 7 =$	$27 \div 9 =$	$72 \div 9 =$
$36 \div 6 =$	$42 \div 7 =$	$54 \div 9 =$	$30 \div 6 =$
$42 \div 6 =$	$16 \div 8 =$	$36 \div 6 =$	$21 \div 7 =$
$32 \div 8 =$	$56 \div 7 =$	$7 \div 7 =$	$90 \div 9 =$
$18 \div 6 =$	$100 \div 10 =$	$35 \div 7 =$	$48 \div 8 =$
$45 \div 9 =$	$36 \div 6 =$	$80 \div 8 =$	$12 \div 6 =$
$100 \div 10 =$	$28 \div 7 =$	$100 \div 10 =$	$9 \div 9 =$
$27 \div 9 =$	$63 \div 9 =$	$18 \div 6 =$	$28 \div 7 =$
$0 \div 9 =$	$40 \div 10 =$	$14 \div 7 =$	$27 \div 9 =$
$80 \div 10 =$	$20 \div 10 =$	$63 \div 9 =$	$80 \div 8 =$
$42 \div 6 =$	$10 \div 10 =$	$81 \div 9 =$	$48 \div 8 =$
$54 \div 6 =$	$90 \div 10 =$	$42 \div 6 =$	$42 \div 7 =$

Time: _____   Score: _____

$0 \div 9 =$	$81 \div 9 =$	$18 \div 9 =$	$36 \div 9 =$
$80 \div 10 =$	$81 \div 9 =$	$56 \div 7 =$	$30 \div 6 =$
$16 \div 8 =$	$27 \div 9 =$	$72 \div 9 =$	$80 \div 10 =$
$70 \div 10 =$	$45 \div 9 =$	$24 \div 6 =$	$42 \div 6 =$
$48 \div 8 =$	$80 \div 8 =$	$0 \div 9 =$	$24 \div 8 =$
$90 \div 9 =$	$42 \div 6 =$	$16 \div 8 =$	$64 \div 8 =$
$14 \div 7 =$	$81 \div 9 =$	$16 \div 8 =$	$36 \div 9 =$
$20 \div 10 =$	$72 \div 8 =$	$80 \div 8 =$	$56 \div 7 =$
$56 \div 8 =$	$32 \div 8 =$	$16 \div 8 =$	$18 \div 9 =$
$63 \div 7 =$	$56 \div 8 =$	$32 \div 8 =$	$30 \div 10 =$
$64 \div 8 =$	$60 \div 10 =$	$36 \div 6 =$	$32 \div 8 =$
$72 \div 9 =$	$27 \div 9 =$	$56 \div 7 =$	$35 \div 7 =$
$80 \div 8 =$	$80 \div 10 =$	$70 \div 10 =$	$0 \div 6 =$
$48 \div 6 =$	$42 \div 6 =$	$54 \div 6 =$	$72 \div 9 =$
$64 \div 8 =$	$81 \div 9 =$	$7 \div 7 =$	$60 \div 10 =$
$48 \div 6 =$	$80 \div 8 =$	$7 \div 7 =$	$90 \div 10 =$
$45 \div 9 =$	$10 \div 10 =$	$30 \div 10 =$	$42 \div 7 =$
$16 \div 8 =$	$72 \div 8 =$	$18 \div 9 =$	$0 \div 6 =$

Time: _____   Score: _____

$70 \div 7 =$	$0 \div 8 =$	$14 \div 7 =$	$30 \div 10 =$
$24 \div 6 =$	$18 \div 9 =$	$6 \div 6 =$	$60 \div 6 =$
$54 \div 9 =$	$63 \div 9 =$	$42 \div 7 =$	$12 \div 6 =$
$90 \div 10 =$	$45 \div 9 =$	$48 \div 8 =$	$40 \div 8 =$
$60 \div 10 =$	$30 \div 10 =$	$18 \div 9 =$	$12 \div 6 =$
$40 \div 8 =$	$56 \div 8 =$	$60 \div 6 =$	$20 \div 10 =$
$63 \div 9 =$	$36 \div 9 =$	$70 \div 7 =$	$42 \div 6 =$
$18 \div 9 =$	$60 \div 6 =$	$0 \div 10 =$	$0 \div 6 =$
$6 \div 6 =$	$40 \div 10 =$	$28 \div 7 =$	$21 \div 7 =$
$45 \div 9 =$	$24 \div 8 =$	$54 \div 9 =$	$0 \div 8 =$
$48 \div 6 =$	$18 \div 9 =$	$60 \div 6 =$	$14 \div 7 =$
$9 \div 9 =$	$30 \div 6 =$	$40 \div 10 =$	$24 \div 6 =$
$32 \div 8 =$	$0 \div 8 =$	$90 \div 9 =$	$80 \div 10 =$
$70 \div 7 =$	$81 \div 9 =$	$60 \div 10 =$	$80 \div 8 =$
$40 \div 10 =$	$40 \div 10 =$	$90 \div 10 =$	$30 \div 10 =$
$45 \div 9 =$	$36 \div 9 =$	$48 \div 8 =$	$28 \div 7 =$
$70 \div 10 =$	$90 \div 10 =$	$100 \div 10 =$	$28 \div 7 =$
$36 \div 6 =$	$90 \div 9 =$	$63 \div 7 =$	$42 \div 7 =$

Time: _____   Score: _____

$24 \div 8 =$	$54 \div 9 =$	$90 \div 10 =$	$27 \div 9 =$
$20 \div 10 =$	$18 \div 6 =$	$36 \div 6 =$	$30 \div 6 =$
$20 \div 10 =$	$0 \div 8 =$	$18 \div 6 =$	$14 \div 7 =$
$0 \div 9 =$	$28 \div 7 =$	$24 \div 6 =$	$16 \div 8 =$
$100 \div 10 =$	$56 \div 7 =$	$0 \div 7 =$	$42 \div 6 =$
$20 \div 10 =$	$0 \div 10 =$	$64 \div 8 =$	$42 \div 7 =$
$24 \div 8 =$	$72 \div 8 =$	$12 \div 6 =$	$35 \div 7 =$
$18 \div 9 =$	$21 \div 7 =$	$7 \div 7 =$	$0 \div 6 =$
$56 \div 7 =$	$6 \div 6 =$	$35 \div 7 =$	$48 \div 8 =$
$0 \div 9 =$	$9 \div 9 =$	$90 \div 9 =$	$30 \div 10 =$
$0 \div 10 =$	$54 \div 6 =$	$20 \div 10 =$	$56 \div 7 =$
$18 \div 9 =$	$32 \div 8 =$	$42 \div 7 =$	$63 \div 7 =$
$30 \div 6 =$	$42 \div 7 =$	$42 \div 6 =$	$9 \div 9 =$
$28 \div 7 =$	$70 \div 10 =$	$50 \div 10 =$	$24 \div 8 =$
$70 \div 10 =$	$36 \div 9 =$	$48 \div 6 =$	$70 \div 7 =$
$28 \div 7 =$	$80 \div 10 =$	$12 \div 6 =$	$30 \div 10 =$
$60 \div 10 =$	$90 \div 10 =$	$48 \div 8 =$	$60 \div 10 =$
$12 \div 6 =$	$6 \div 6 =$	$0 \div 10 =$	$42 \div 7 =$

Time: _____   Score: _____

24 ÷ 6 =	21 ÷ 7 =	42 ÷ 7 =	81 ÷ 9 =
0 ÷ 10 =	40 ÷ 10 =	18 ÷ 9 =	8 ÷ 8 =
18 ÷ 6 =	18 ÷ 9 =	80 ÷ 8 =	48 ÷ 6 =
80 ÷ 10 =	60 ÷ 10 =	0 ÷ 7 =	21 ÷ 7 =
32 ÷ 8 =	70 ÷ 10 =	35 ÷ 7 =	0 ÷ 6 =
30 ÷ 6 =	49 ÷ 7 =	54 ÷ 9 =	45 ÷ 9 =
90 ÷ 9 =	20 ÷ 10 =	30 ÷ 6 =	60 ÷ 6 =
9 ÷ 9 =	54 ÷ 6 =	90 ÷ 9 =	30 ÷ 6 =
48 ÷ 8 =	28 ÷ 7 =	48 ÷ 6 =	36 ÷ 6 =
80 ÷ 8 =	0 ÷ 10 =	50 ÷ 10 =	0 ÷ 10 =
90 ÷ 9 =	72 ÷ 8 =	63 ÷ 9 =	18 ÷ 6 =
30 ÷ 6 =	28 ÷ 7 =	18 ÷ 9 =	64 ÷ 8 =
35 ÷ 7 =	12 ÷ 6 =	63 ÷ 9 =	81 ÷ 9 =
50 ÷ 10 =	0 ÷ 7 =	18 ÷ 6 =	56 ÷ 8 =
45 ÷ 9 =	14 ÷ 7 =	40 ÷ 10 =	72 ÷ 9 =
63 ÷ 9 =	50 ÷ 10 =	63 ÷ 9 =	12 ÷ 6 =
60 ÷ 10 =	9 ÷ 9 =	48 ÷ 8 =	30 ÷ 10 =
60 ÷ 10 =	14 ÷ 7 =	18 ÷ 6 =	7 ÷ 7 =

Time: _____   Score: _____

80 ÷ 8 =	48 ÷ 6 =	40 ÷ 8 =	10 ÷ 10 =
12 ÷ 6 =	63 ÷ 7 =	63 ÷ 9 =	72 ÷ 9 =
10 ÷ 10 =	28 ÷ 7 =	14 ÷ 7 =	16 ÷ 8 =
42 ÷ 6 =	70 ÷ 10 =	9 ÷ 9 =	72 ÷ 8 =
30 ÷ 6 =	14 ÷ 7 =	32 ÷ 8 =	48 ÷ 8 =
10 ÷ 10 =	63 ÷ 7 =	56 ÷ 8 =	27 ÷ 9 =
12 ÷ 6 =	36 ÷ 9 =	49 ÷ 7 =	100 ÷ 10 =
14 ÷ 7 =	10 ÷ 10 =	6 ÷ 6 =	18 ÷ 6 =
70 ÷ 10 =	48 ÷ 8 =	30 ÷ 10 =	27 ÷ 9 =
9 ÷ 9 =	70 ÷ 10 =	6 ÷ 6 =	6 ÷ 6 =
70 ÷ 10 =	14 ÷ 7 =	90 ÷ 9 =	14 ÷ 7 =
21 ÷ 7 =	45 ÷ 9 =	42 ÷ 7 =	70 ÷ 10 =
0 ÷ 10 =	24 ÷ 6 =	30 ÷ 6 =	40 ÷ 8 =
70 ÷ 7 =	56 ÷ 8 =	9 ÷ 9 =	36 ÷ 9 =
80 ÷ 10 =	50 ÷ 10 =	7 ÷ 7 =	0 ÷ 9 =
72 ÷ 8 =	35 ÷ 7 =	0 ÷ 8 =	16 ÷ 8 =
42 ÷ 6 =	0 ÷ 8 =	7 ÷ 7 =	27 ÷ 9 =
6 ÷ 6 =	70 ÷ 10 =	70 ÷ 10 =	81 ÷ 9 =

Time: _____   Score: _____

0 ÷ 9 =	0 ÷ 7 =	7 ÷ 7 =	81 ÷ 9 =
72 ÷ 9 =	56 ÷ 8 =	81 ÷ 9 =	45 ÷ 9 =
70 ÷ 7 =	48 ÷ 6 =	10 ÷ 10 =	81 ÷ 9 =
56 ÷ 7 =	0 ÷ 6 =	10 ÷ 10 =	0 ÷ 9 =
70 ÷ 7 =	9 ÷ 9 =	36 ÷ 9 =	64 ÷ 8 =
6 ÷ 6 =	24 ÷ 8 =	48 ÷ 6 =	36 ÷ 9 =
16 ÷ 8 =	14 ÷ 7 =	54 ÷ 9 =	48 ÷ 6 =
18 ÷ 9 =	21 ÷ 7 =	30 ÷ 10 =	48 ÷ 8 =
72 ÷ 8 =	50 ÷ 10 =	27 ÷ 9 =	64 ÷ 8 =
56 ÷ 8 =	72 ÷ 9 =	40 ÷ 8 =	72 ÷ 9 =
24 ÷ 8 =	70 ÷ 10 =	60 ÷ 10 =	0 ÷ 9 =
80 ÷ 8 =	21 ÷ 7 =	72 ÷ 8 =	48 ÷ 8 =
42 ÷ 7 =	0 ÷ 8 =	16 ÷ 8 =	21 ÷ 7 =
70 ÷ 10 =	90 ÷ 9 =	70 ÷ 10 =	9 ÷ 9 =
72 ÷ 9 =	70 ÷ 10 =	60 ÷ 10 =	90 ÷ 9 =
100 ÷ 10 =	12 ÷ 6 =	80 ÷ 8 =	16 ÷ 8 =
42 ÷ 7 =	48 ÷ 8 =	18 ÷ 9 =	64 ÷ 8 =
14 ÷ 7 =	28 ÷ 7 =	16 ÷ 8 =	90 ÷ 10 =

Time: _____   Score: _____

$72 \div 9 =$	$9 \div 9 =$	$0 \div 7 =$	$30 \div 6 =$
$63 \div 9 =$	$54 \div 9 =$	$42 \div 7 =$	$70 \div 10 =$
$0 \div 10 =$	$7 \div 7 =$	$8 \div 8 =$	$48 \div 8 =$
$72 \div 9 =$	$56 \div 8 =$	$50 \div 10 =$	$24 \div 6 =$
$81 \div 9 =$	$18 \div 9 =$	$100 \div 10 =$	$24 \div 8 =$
$14 \div 7 =$	$21 \div 7 =$	$0 \div 7 =$	$40 \div 10 =$
$80 \div 10 =$	$45 \div 9 =$	$18 \div 9 =$	$56 \div 7 =$
$18 \div 6 =$	$7 \div 7 =$	$63 \div 7 =$	$7 \div 7 =$
$35 \div 7 =$	$40 \div 8 =$	$8 \div 8 =$	$20 \div 10 =$
$63 \div 7 =$	$27 \div 9 =$	$42 \div 6 =$	$48 \div 6 =$
$12 \div 6 =$	$72 \div 8 =$	$9 \div 9 =$	$49 \div 7 =$
$30 \div 6 =$	$24 \div 6 =$	$60 \div 10 =$	$70 \div 7 =$
$24 \div 6 =$	$27 \div 9 =$	$0 \div 8 =$	$70 \div 10 =$
$72 \div 9 =$	$48 \div 6 =$	$42 \div 7 =$	$45 \div 9 =$
$70 \div 7 =$	$42 \div 7 =$	$63 \div 9 =$	$24 \div 8 =$
$32 \div 8 =$	$36 \div 9 =$	$24 \div 8 =$	$60 \div 10 =$
$30 \div 6 =$	$54 \div 9 =$	$30 \div 6 =$	$18 \div 9 =$
$80 \div 8 =$	$90 \div 9 =$	$42 \div 6 =$	$40 \div 10 =$

Time: _____   Score: _____

0 ÷ 8 =	54 ÷ 9 =	80 ÷ 10 =	63 ÷ 7 =
35 ÷ 7 =	24 ÷ 8 =	0 ÷ 7 =	63 ÷ 7 =
90 ÷ 9 =	36 ÷ 9 =	70 ÷ 10 =	50 ÷ 10 =
64 ÷ 8 =	28 ÷ 7 =	7 ÷ 7 =	63 ÷ 7 =
64 ÷ 8 =	60 ÷ 6 =	30 ÷ 6 =	49 ÷ 7 =
81 ÷ 9 =	36 ÷ 9 =	64 ÷ 8 =	48 ÷ 6 =
21 ÷ 7 =	18 ÷ 6 =	27 ÷ 9 =	28 ÷ 7 =
40 ÷ 8 =	90 ÷ 9 =	21 ÷ 7 =	60 ÷ 6 =
0 ÷ 8 =	63 ÷ 7 =	60 ÷ 10 =	16 ÷ 8 =
80 ÷ 10 =	40 ÷ 8 =	7 ÷ 7 =	50 ÷ 10 =
56 ÷ 7 =	56 ÷ 7 =	24 ÷ 6 =	90 ÷ 10 =
6 ÷ 6 =	64 ÷ 8 =	27 ÷ 9 =	81 ÷ 9 =
0 ÷ 7 =	40 ÷ 10 =	63 ÷ 9 =	60 ÷ 10 =
14 ÷ 7 =	100 ÷ 10 =	80 ÷ 8 =	18 ÷ 6 =
21 ÷ 7 =	24 ÷ 6 =	48 ÷ 8 =	56 ÷ 8 =
60 ÷ 10 =	24 ÷ 8 =	20 ÷ 10 =	28 ÷ 7 =
36 ÷ 6 =	12 ÷ 6 =	70 ÷ 7 =	63 ÷ 9 =
18 ÷ 9 =	40 ÷ 8 =	40 ÷ 10 =	21 ÷ 7 =

Time: _____   Score: _____

$63 \div 9 =$	$48 \div 8 =$	$90 \div 9 =$	$49 \div 7 =$
$27 \div 9 =$	$9 \div 9 =$	$32 \div 8 =$	$18 \div 9 =$
$0 \div 7 =$	$10 \div 10 =$	$63 \div 9 =$	$40 \div 10 =$
$60 \div 6 =$	$9 \div 9 =$	$60 \div 6 =$	$72 \div 9 =$
$6 \div 6 =$	$27 \div 9 =$	$90 \div 10 =$	$35 \div 7 =$
$0 \div 9 =$	$14 \div 7 =$	$50 \div 10 =$	$48 \div 6 =$
$18 \div 6 =$	$30 \div 6 =$	$20 \div 10 =$	$30 \div 10 =$
$32 \div 8 =$	$36 \div 9 =$	$0 \div 6 =$	$10 \div 10 =$
$21 \div 7 =$	$100 \div 10 =$	$40 \div 8 =$	$49 \div 7 =$
$30 \div 6 =$	$70 \div 10 =$	$100 \div 10 =$	$30 \div 10 =$
$80 \div 8 =$	$12 \div 6 =$	$10 \div 10 =$	$45 \div 9 =$
$20 \div 10 =$	$14 \div 7 =$	$81 \div 9 =$	$12 \div 6 =$
$0 \div 10 =$	$12 \div 6 =$	$54 \div 9 =$	$42 \div 7 =$
$0 \div 6 =$	$63 \div 9 =$	$63 \div 9 =$	$80 \div 8 =$
$14 \div 7 =$	$40 \div 10 =$	$30 \div 10 =$	$56 \div 8 =$
$54 \div 9 =$	$72 \div 9 =$	$56 \div 8 =$	$60 \div 10 =$
$20 \div 10 =$	$40 \div 10 =$	$28 \div 7 =$	$7 \div 7 =$
$6 \div 6 =$	$49 \div 7 =$	$72 \div 8 =$	$48 \div 6 =$

Time: _____   Score: _____

35 ÷ 7 =	50 ÷ 10 =	28 ÷ 7 =	21 ÷ 7 =
54 ÷ 9 =	60 ÷ 10 =	90 ÷ 9 =	28 ÷ 7 =
10 ÷ 10 =	28 ÷ 7 =	72 ÷ 9 =	60 ÷ 6 =
14 ÷ 7 =	56 ÷ 7 =	14 ÷ 7 =	72 ÷ 9 =
100 ÷ 10 =	70 ÷ 10 =	18 ÷ 6 =	42 ÷ 6 =
27 ÷ 9 =	8 ÷ 8 =	54 ÷ 6 =	40 ÷ 8 =
100 ÷ 10 =	54 ÷ 9 =	42 ÷ 7 =	56 ÷ 8 =
90 ÷ 10 =	90 ÷ 9 =	18 ÷ 6 =	64 ÷ 8 =
63 ÷ 9 =	32 ÷ 8 =	24 ÷ 8 =	63 ÷ 9 =
24 ÷ 8 =	64 ÷ 8 =	0 ÷ 10 =	0 ÷ 10 =
72 ÷ 8 =	18 ÷ 9 =	80 ÷ 8 =	6 ÷ 6 =
45 ÷ 9 =	0 ÷ 6 =	24 ÷ 6 =	60 ÷ 10 =
40 ÷ 8 =	18 ÷ 6 =	49 ÷ 7 =	16 ÷ 8 =
10 ÷ 10 =	0 ÷ 10 =	56 ÷ 7 =	60 ÷ 10 =
40 ÷ 8 =	35 ÷ 7 =	80 ÷ 8 =	36 ÷ 6 =
0 ÷ 6 =	8 ÷ 8 =	60 ÷ 10 =	8 ÷ 8 =
70 ÷ 7 =	64 ÷ 8 =	10 ÷ 10 =	0 ÷ 8 =
48 ÷ 8 =	63 ÷ 7 =	90 ÷ 10 =	0 ÷ 10 =

Time: _____   Score: _____

0 ÷ 7 =	60 ÷ 10 =	30 ÷ 10 =	63 ÷ 9 =
24 ÷ 8 =	10 ÷ 10 =	40 ÷ 8 =	30 ÷ 10 =
28 ÷ 7 =	40 ÷ 10 =	0 ÷ 8 =	70 ÷ 10 =
40 ÷ 10 =	90 ÷ 10 =	36 ÷ 6 =	54 ÷ 6 =
30 ÷ 10 =	80 ÷ 10 =	60 ÷ 10 =	36 ÷ 6 =
54 ÷ 9 =	40 ÷ 8 =	18 ÷ 6 =	0 ÷ 8 =
12 ÷ 6 =	42 ÷ 7 =	81 ÷ 9 =	10 ÷ 10 =
21 ÷ 7 =	63 ÷ 7 =	40 ÷ 8 =	72 ÷ 9 =
70 ÷ 7 =	72 ÷ 9 =	6 ÷ 6 =	0 ÷ 9 =
81 ÷ 9 =	27 ÷ 9 =	80 ÷ 8 =	60 ÷ 6 =
18 ÷ 9 =	30 ÷ 10 =	30 ÷ 6 =	100 ÷ 10 =
36 ÷ 6 =	30 ÷ 6 =	81 ÷ 9 =	0 ÷ 9 =
36 ÷ 6 =	90 ÷ 9 =	0 ÷ 7 =	80 ÷ 10 =
32 ÷ 8 =	27 ÷ 9 =	40 ÷ 10 =	40 ÷ 10 =
81 ÷ 9 =	0 ÷ 7 =	36 ÷ 9 =	54 ÷ 9 =
36 ÷ 9 =	48 ÷ 8 =	12 ÷ 6 =	35 ÷ 7 =
60 ÷ 6 =	63 ÷ 9 =	0 ÷ 8 =	72 ÷ 8 =
18 ÷ 9 =	63 ÷ 7 =	36 ÷ 9 =	0 ÷ 7 =

Time: _____   Score: _____

$12 \div 6 =$	$49 \div 7 =$	$27 \div 9 =$	$35 \div 7 =$
$48 \div 6 =$	$9 \div 9 =$	$35 \div 7 =$	$70 \div 10 =$
$49 \div 7 =$	$24 \div 6 =$	$70 \div 10 =$	$10 \div 10 =$
$20 \div 10 =$	$30 \div 10 =$	$50 \div 10 =$	$36 \div 9 =$
$60 \div 6 =$	$50 \div 10 =$	$45 \div 9 =$	$30 \div 10 =$
$100 \div 10 =$	$32 \div 8 =$	$14 \div 7 =$	$40 \div 10 =$
$18 \div 6 =$	$80 \div 10 =$	$81 \div 9 =$	$35 \div 7 =$
$48 \div 6 =$	$45 \div 9 =$	$8 \div 8 =$	$56 \div 7 =$
$40 \div 8 =$	$54 \div 9 =$	$24 \div 8 =$	$0 \div 6 =$
$0 \div 6 =$	$9 \div 9 =$	$45 \div 9 =$	$30 \div 6 =$
$42 \div 6 =$	$90 \div 9 =$	$24 \div 8 =$	$70 \div 7 =$
$32 \div 8 =$	$14 \div 7 =$	$64 \div 8 =$	$10 \div 10 =$
$0 \div 10 =$	$8 \div 8 =$	$80 \div 8 =$	$50 \div 10 =$
$54 \div 9 =$	$0 \div 6 =$	$48 \div 8 =$	$80 \div 10 =$
$50 \div 10 =$	$16 \div 8 =$	$54 \div 6 =$	$30 \div 10 =$
$81 \div 9 =$	$6 \div 6 =$	$24 \div 6 =$	$48 \div 6 =$
$72 \div 9 =$	$40 \div 8 =$	$60 \div 6 =$	$81 \div 9 =$
$0 \div 6 =$	$50 \div 10 =$	$48 \div 8 =$	$40 \div 8 =$

Time: _____   Score: _____

80 ÷ 10 =	54 ÷ 9 =	28 ÷ 7 =	9 ÷ 9 =
56 ÷ 8 =	60 ÷ 6 =	40 ÷ 10 =	56 ÷ 8 =
9 ÷ 9 =	70 ÷ 10 =	72 ÷ 9 =	20 ÷ 10 =
20 ÷ 10 =	10 ÷ 10 =	21 ÷ 7 =	18 ÷ 9 =
30 ÷ 6 =	56 ÷ 8 =	6 ÷ 6 =	20 ÷ 10 =
40 ÷ 8 =	63 ÷ 9 =	60 ÷ 10 =	63 ÷ 9 =
14 ÷ 7 =	49 ÷ 7 =	40 ÷ 8 =	36 ÷ 9 =
20 ÷ 10 =	90 ÷ 10 =	54 ÷ 9 =	21 ÷ 7 =
56 ÷ 7 =	81 ÷ 9 =	54 ÷ 9 =	63 ÷ 7 =
49 ÷ 7 =	90 ÷ 10 =	12 ÷ 6 =	56 ÷ 8 =
18 ÷ 9 =	30 ÷ 10 =	27 ÷ 9 =	49 ÷ 7 =
70 ÷ 10 =	36 ÷ 6 =	72 ÷ 8 =	0 ÷ 7 =
0 ÷ 6 =	90 ÷ 10 =	90 ÷ 10 =	16 ÷ 8 =
32 ÷ 8 =	0 ÷ 6 =	10 ÷ 10 =	81 ÷ 9 =
60 ÷ 6 =	0 ÷ 8 =	18 ÷ 9 =	7 ÷ 7 =
36 ÷ 6 =	0 ÷ 6 =	60 ÷ 10 =	36 ÷ 9 =
80 ÷ 10 =	72 ÷ 9 =	72 ÷ 8 =	70 ÷ 10 =
63 ÷ 7 =	0 ÷ 10 =	45 ÷ 9 =	54 ÷ 9 =

Time: _____   Score: _____

30 ÷ 6 =	80 ÷ 10 =	64 ÷ 8 =	30 ÷ 10 =
18 ÷ 9 =	56 ÷ 7 =	24 ÷ 6 =	24 ÷ 8 =
56 ÷ 8 =	36 ÷ 9 =	27 ÷ 9 =	48 ÷ 8 =
30 ÷ 10 =	63 ÷ 9 =	70 ÷ 10 =	0 ÷ 9 =
48 ÷ 8 =	90 ÷ 10 =	40 ÷ 8 =	14 ÷ 7 =
0 ÷ 6 =	24 ÷ 8 =	35 ÷ 7 =	0 ÷ 6 =
70 ÷ 10 =	21 ÷ 7 =	7 ÷ 7 =	0 ÷ 6 =
14 ÷ 7 =	49 ÷ 7 =	24 ÷ 6 =	21 ÷ 7 =
56 ÷ 8 =	0 ÷ 6 =	40 ÷ 8 =	28 ÷ 7 =
0 ÷ 9 =	42 ÷ 6 =	42 ÷ 6 =	20 ÷ 10 =
9 ÷ 9 =	63 ÷ 9 =	40 ÷ 10 =	36 ÷ 9 =
56 ÷ 8 =	36 ÷ 6 =	20 ÷ 10 =	90 ÷ 10 =
35 ÷ 7 =	32 ÷ 8 =	24 ÷ 6 =	48 ÷ 6 =
30 ÷ 6 =	50 ÷ 10 =	90 ÷ 10 =	24 ÷ 8 =
90 ÷ 9 =	27 ÷ 9 =	32 ÷ 8 =	64 ÷ 8 =
64 ÷ 8 =	80 ÷ 10 =	14 ÷ 7 =	81 ÷ 9 =
72 ÷ 8 =	80 ÷ 8 =	90 ÷ 10 =	12 ÷ 6 =
9 ÷ 9 =	63 ÷ 7 =	30 ÷ 10 =	10 ÷ 10 =

Time: _____   Score: _____

90 ÷ 10 =	45 ÷ 9 =	12 ÷ 6 =	18 ÷ 6 =
70 ÷ 10 =	0 ÷ 10 =	18 ÷ 6 =	80 ÷ 10 =
70 ÷ 7 =	0 ÷ 10 =	100 ÷ 10 =	63 ÷ 7 =
28 ÷ 7 =	0 ÷ 9 =	63 ÷ 7 =	40 ÷ 10 =
90 ÷ 9 =	80 ÷ 8 =	54 ÷ 6 =	81 ÷ 9 =
32 ÷ 8 =	48 ÷ 8 =	7 ÷ 7 =	12 ÷ 6 =
40 ÷ 8 =	40 ÷ 8 =	49 ÷ 7 =	54 ÷ 6 =
30 ÷ 10 =	48 ÷ 8 =	80 ÷ 8 =	0 ÷ 6 =
42 ÷ 7 =	40 ÷ 8 =	20 ÷ 10 =	90 ÷ 9 =
30 ÷ 10 =	0 ÷ 7 =	27 ÷ 9 =	45 ÷ 9 =
56 ÷ 8 =	30 ÷ 6 =	49 ÷ 7 =	90 ÷ 10 =
49 ÷ 7 =	49 ÷ 7 =	0 ÷ 6 =	50 ÷ 10 =
70 ÷ 10 =	0 ÷ 8 =	16 ÷ 8 =	0 ÷ 10 =
27 ÷ 9 =	40 ÷ 10 =	56 ÷ 8 =	12 ÷ 6 =
42 ÷ 6 =	54 ÷ 6 =	28 ÷ 7 =	16 ÷ 8 =
30 ÷ 6 =	42 ÷ 6 =	30 ÷ 10 =	0 ÷ 7 =
63 ÷ 9 =	36 ÷ 6 =	63 ÷ 9 =	21 ÷ 7 =
0 ÷ 9 =	7 ÷ 7 =	24 ÷ 6 =	40 ÷ 8 =

Part 4: Practice Mixed Division Facts up to Ten

Time: _____   Score: _____

0 ÷ 4 =	50 ÷ 5 =	0 ÷ 9 =	4 ÷ 1 =
10 ÷ 10 =	32 ÷ 4 =	32 ÷ 8 =	1 ÷ 1 =
18 ÷ 9 =	18 ÷ 6 =	12 ÷ 3 =	35 ÷ 7 =
56 ÷ 7 =	30 ÷ 3 =	30 ÷ 10 =	50 ÷ 10 =
64 ÷ 8 =	64 ÷ 8 =	80 ÷ 10 =	24 ÷ 4 =
70 ÷ 10 =	48 ÷ 6 =	80 ÷ 8 =	40 ÷ 5 =
12 ÷ 3 =	45 ÷ 9 =	0 ÷ 9 =	4 ÷ 1 =
27 ÷ 3 =	32 ÷ 8 =	0 ÷ 2 =	25 ÷ 5 =
50 ÷ 5 =	10 ÷ 2 =	20 ÷ 10 =	15 ÷ 3 =
18 ÷ 2 =	6 ÷ 3 =	45 ÷ 9 =	40 ÷ 10 =
18 ÷ 6 =	12 ÷ 3 =	24 ÷ 8 =	20 ÷ 2 =
4 ÷ 2 =	20 ÷ 2 =	8 ÷ 1 =	8 ÷ 2 =
90 ÷ 9 =	0 ÷ 6 =	63 ÷ 9 =	24 ÷ 8 =
24 ÷ 4 =	10 ÷ 1 =	56 ÷ 8 =	0 ÷ 1 =
3 ÷ 3 =	36 ÷ 6 =	63 ÷ 7 =	21 ÷ 7 =
72 ÷ 8 =	18 ÷ 6 =	64 ÷ 8 =	24 ÷ 8 =
45 ÷ 9 =	0 ÷ 2 =	63 ÷ 7 =	12 ÷ 6 =

Time: _____   Score: _____

21 ÷ 3 =	10 ÷ 5 =	30 ÷ 3 =	100 ÷ 10 =
12 ÷ 2 =	16 ÷ 8 =	16 ÷ 2 =	35 ÷ 5 =
90 ÷ 10 =	28 ÷ 7 =	0 ÷ 7 =	0 ÷ 1 =
2 ÷ 1 =	0 ÷ 4 =	36 ÷ 9 =	2 ÷ 1 =
9 ÷ 3 =	28 ÷ 4 =	25 ÷ 5 =	24 ÷ 3 =
72 ÷ 8 =	45 ÷ 5 =	0 ÷ 1 =	16 ÷ 4 =
70 ÷ 10 =	80 ÷ 10 =	90 ÷ 9 =	20 ÷ 2 =
14 ÷ 7 =	56 ÷ 7 =	16 ÷ 8 =	36 ÷ 4 =
5 ÷ 5 =	0 ÷ 10 =	6 ÷ 6 =	28 ÷ 7 =
5 ÷ 5 =	90 ÷ 10 =	45 ÷ 9 =	45 ÷ 5 =
15 ÷ 5 =	2 ÷ 2 =	20 ÷ 2 =	81 ÷ 9 =
80 ÷ 10 =	70 ÷ 10 =	5 ÷ 5 =	12 ÷ 4 =
2 ÷ 2 =	7 ÷ 7 =	70 ÷ 10 =	70 ÷ 7 =
60 ÷ 6 =	49 ÷ 7 =	81 ÷ 9 =	24 ÷ 3 =
18 ÷ 2 =	50 ÷ 10 =	56 ÷ 8 =	45 ÷ 9 =
30 ÷ 3 =	0 ÷ 5 =	4 ÷ 4 =	0 ÷ 8 =
30 ÷ 6 =	0 ÷ 8 =	24 ÷ 6 =	12 ÷ 3 =
54 ÷ 6 =	9 ÷ 3 =	36 ÷ 9 =	54 ÷ 9 =

Time: _____   Score: _____

30 ÷ 5 =	16 ÷ 4 =	35 ÷ 7 =	14 ÷ 7 =
21 ÷ 7 =	18 ÷ 9 =	16 ÷ 2 =	54 ÷ 9 =
8 ÷ 4 =	90 ÷ 9 =	100 ÷ 10 =	20 ÷ 2 =
32 ÷ 8 =	63 ÷ 9 =	16 ÷ 8 =	18 ÷ 3 =
30 ÷ 3 =	28 ÷ 4 =	27 ÷ 9 =	90 ÷ 10 =
45 ÷ 5 =	36 ÷ 6 =	81 ÷ 9 =	48 ÷ 8 =
0 ÷ 2 =	48 ÷ 6 =	56 ÷ 7 =	3 ÷ 3 =
30 ÷ 3 =	0 ÷ 6 =	72 ÷ 9 =	14 ÷ 2 =
60 ÷ 10 =	63 ÷ 9 =	8 ÷ 8 =	12 ÷ 4 =
24 ÷ 3 =	90 ÷ 10 =	45 ÷ 5 =	64 ÷ 8 =
24 ÷ 3 =	12 ÷ 4 =	15 ÷ 5 =	28 ÷ 4 =
1 ÷ 1 =	35 ÷ 5 =	32 ÷ 4 =	4 ÷ 2 =
9 ÷ 1 =	0 ÷ 9 =	4 ÷ 2 =	18 ÷ 6 =
12 ÷ 2 =	18 ÷ 9 =	35 ÷ 7 =	9 ÷ 9 =
21 ÷ 3 =	50 ÷ 5 =	5 ÷ 1 =	48 ÷ 8 =
42 ÷ 7 =	56 ÷ 7 =	80 ÷ 10 =	10 ÷ 5 =
30 ÷ 10 =	60 ÷ 10 =	4 ÷ 4 =	5 ÷ 5 =
42 ÷ 6 =	45 ÷ 5 =	9 ÷ 9 =	3 ÷ 1 =

Time: _____   Score: _____

$32 \div 8 =$	$0 \div 1 =$	$0 \div 10 =$	$60 \div 6 =$
$20 \div 5 =$	$50 \div 10 =$	$18 \div 2 =$	$18 \div 3 =$
$7 \div 1 =$	$45 \div 5 =$	$18 \div 3 =$	$16 \div 2 =$
$60 \div 6 =$	$80 \div 10 =$	$9 \div 3 =$	$28 \div 4 =$
$20 \div 10 =$	$70 \div 10 =$	$40 \div 10 =$	$2 \div 1 =$
$2 \div 1 =$	$45 \div 5 =$	$8 \div 1 =$	$49 \div 7 =$
$42 \div 6 =$	$24 \div 4 =$	$14 \div 2 =$	$14 \div 7 =$
$42 \div 7 =$	$4 \div 1 =$	$0 \div 10 =$	$12 \div 3 =$
$0 \div 9 =$	$9 \div 3 =$	$30 \div 3 =$	$35 \div 7 =$
$4 \div 2 =$	$49 \div 7 =$	$30 \div 5 =$	$0 \div 2 =$
$8 \div 1 =$	$0 \div 6 =$	$35 \div 7 =$	$28 \div 7 =$
$1 \div 1 =$	$0 \div 7 =$	$90 \div 10 =$	$0 \div 1 =$
$7 \div 7 =$	$36 \div 9 =$	$24 \div 3 =$	$0 \div 5 =$
$30 \div 5 =$	$63 \div 9 =$	$7 \div 7 =$	$12 \div 3 =$
$27 \div 3 =$	$2 \div 1 =$	$0 \div 8 =$	$30 \div 10 =$
$8 \div 1 =$	$8 \div 1 =$	$8 \div 8 =$	$12 \div 4 =$
$42 \div 6 =$	$36 \div 4 =$	$70 \div 10 =$	$90 \div 9 =$
$32 \div 8 =$	$3 \div 1 =$	$0 \div 1 =$	$48 \div 6 =$

Time: _____   Score: _____

24 ÷ 6 =	54 ÷ 9 =	40 ÷ 5 =	8 ÷ 8 =
21 ÷ 7 =	4 ÷ 2 =	56 ÷ 7 =	60 ÷ 6 =
64 ÷ 8 =	6 ÷ 2 =	81 ÷ 9 =	90 ÷ 9 =
5 ÷ 1 =	20 ÷ 2 =	56 ÷ 8 =	0 ÷ 7 =
16 ÷ 4 =	2 ÷ 2 =	14 ÷ 2 =	36 ÷ 9 =
2 ÷ 2 =	0 ÷ 9 =	20 ÷ 10 =	42 ÷ 7 =
0 ÷ 3 =	18 ÷ 9 =	21 ÷ 3 =	18 ÷ 3 =
10 ÷ 2 =	10 ÷ 5 =	12 ÷ 2 =	15 ÷ 5 =
45 ÷ 5 =	16 ÷ 2 =	40 ÷ 8 =	10 ÷ 10 =
40 ÷ 8 =	15 ÷ 5 =	0 ÷ 4 =	10 ÷ 1 =
20 ÷ 4 =	72 ÷ 9 =	63 ÷ 7 =	72 ÷ 9 =
36 ÷ 4 =	0 ÷ 7 =	5 ÷ 5 =	16 ÷ 8 =
56 ÷ 8 =	64 ÷ 8 =	35 ÷ 7 =	12 ÷ 6 =
0 ÷ 2 =	60 ÷ 10 =	18 ÷ 3 =	40 ÷ 10 =
5 ÷ 1 =	50 ÷ 10 =	0 ÷ 10 =	9 ÷ 3 =
35 ÷ 7 =	48 ÷ 8 =	0 ÷ 6 =	30 ÷ 10 =
0 ÷ 6 =	40 ÷ 10 =	30 ÷ 6 =	28 ÷ 7 =
9 ÷ 3 =	40 ÷ 8 =	6 ÷ 6 =	32 ÷ 8 =

Time: _____   Score: _____

21 ÷ 3 =	42 ÷ 6 =	0 ÷ 1 =	1 ÷ 1 =
8 ÷ 2 =	24 ÷ 8 =	20 ÷ 5 =	48 ÷ 6 =
36 ÷ 9 =	9 ÷ 9 =	2 ÷ 1 =	63 ÷ 7 =
64 ÷ 8 =	9 ÷ 9 =	48 ÷ 8 =	6 ÷ 2 =
80 ÷ 10 =	24 ÷ 3 =	50 ÷ 5 =	30 ÷ 10 =
20 ÷ 4 =	40 ÷ 8 =	15 ÷ 5 =	20 ÷ 2 =
20 ÷ 4 =	0 ÷ 2 =	18 ÷ 6 =	36 ÷ 9 =
16 ÷ 8 =	14 ÷ 2 =	90 ÷ 9 =	9 ÷ 3 =
60 ÷ 6 =	5 ÷ 5 =	12 ÷ 4 =	30 ÷ 6 =
40 ÷ 4 =	6 ÷ 1 =	36 ÷ 6 =	50 ÷ 5 =
3 ÷ 1 =	15 ÷ 5 =	20 ÷ 10 =	45 ÷ 9 =
21 ÷ 3 =	48 ÷ 8 =	14 ÷ 7 =	10 ÷ 1 =
81 ÷ 9 =	36 ÷ 6 =	3 ÷ 3 =	15 ÷ 5 =
6 ÷ 2 =	0 ÷ 3 =	30 ÷ 3 =	7 ÷ 1 =
7 ÷ 7 =	60 ÷ 10 =	54 ÷ 6 =	8 ÷ 1 =
0 ÷ 4 =	12 ÷ 4 =	32 ÷ 8 =	24 ÷ 4 =
20 ÷ 10 =	40 ÷ 5 =	72 ÷ 8 =	5 ÷ 1 =
0 ÷ 2 =	27 ÷ 9 =	4 ÷ 4 =	4 ÷ 4 =

Time: _____   Score: _____

$30 \div 3 =$	$10 \div 5 =$	$63 \div 9 =$	$2 \div 2 =$
$20 \div 10 =$	$30 \div 3 =$	$0 \div 3 =$	$0 \div 1 =$
$36 \div 4 =$	$8 \div 1 =$	$6 \div 2 =$	$27 \div 9 =$
$100 \div 10 =$	$30 \div 10 =$	$5 \div 1 =$	$42 \div 7 =$
$20 \div 5 =$	$35 \div 5 =$	$15 \div 3 =$	$20 \div 4 =$
$56 \div 7 =$	$2 \div 2 =$	$0 \div 1 =$	$0 \div 6 =$
$40 \div 4 =$	$56 \div 8 =$	$49 \div 7 =$	$90 \div 10 =$
$8 \div 1 =$	$3 \div 3 =$	$8 \div 8 =$	$48 \div 6 =$
$0 \div 10 =$	$3 \div 3 =$	$80 \div 10 =$	$0 \div 7 =$
$35 \div 7 =$	$0 \div 10 =$	$63 \div 9 =$	$4 \div 2 =$
$5 \div 1 =$	$3 \div 1 =$	$80 \div 10 =$	$0 \div 6 =$
$48 \div 6 =$	$54 \div 9 =$	$6 \div 1 =$	$6 \div 2 =$
$70 \div 10 =$	$18 \div 3 =$	$72 \div 9 =$	$56 \div 7 =$
$40 \div 10 =$	$5 \div 1 =$	$42 \div 7 =$	$90 \div 10 =$
$3 \div 1 =$	$50 \div 10 =$	$16 \div 8 =$	$32 \div 8 =$
$81 \div 9 =$	$40 \div 8 =$	$24 \div 4 =$	$36 \div 6 =$
$0 \div 7 =$	$4 \div 2 =$	$5 \div 5 =$	$14 \div 2 =$
$20 \div 2 =$	$90 \div 10 =$	$18 \div 9 =$	$18 \div 6 =$

Time: _____   Score: _____

$12 \div 3 =$	$0 \div 9 =$	$12 \div 4 =$	$0 \div 5 =$
$60 \div 6 =$	$16 \div 4 =$	$81 \div 9 =$	$18 \div 2 =$
$10 \div 5 =$	$24 \div 6 =$	$24 \div 4 =$	$16 \div 4 =$
$54 \div 9 =$	$40 \div 4 =$	$70 \div 10 =$	$8 \div 4 =$
$12 \div 6 =$	$40 \div 10 =$	$6 \div 1 =$	$80 \div 8 =$
$0 \div 2 =$	$24 \div 6 =$	$20 \div 5 =$	$9 \div 3 =$
$5 \div 5 =$	$15 \div 3 =$	$54 \div 6 =$	$49 \div 7 =$
$6 \div 2 =$	$15 \div 5 =$	$80 \div 10 =$	$21 \div 3 =$
$20 \div 4 =$	$18 \div 3 =$	$36 \div 6 =$	$70 \div 10 =$
$36 \div 4 =$	$0 \div 6 =$	$14 \div 7 =$	$90 \div 10 =$
$81 \div 9 =$	$56 \div 7 =$	$28 \div 4 =$	$81 \div 9 =$
$0 \div 1 =$	$80 \div 10 =$	$80 \div 10 =$	$25 \div 5 =$
$40 \div 5 =$	$0 \div 4 =$	$0 \div 8 =$	$30 \div 6 =$
$6 \div 1 =$	$24 \div 6 =$	$24 \div 6 =$	$56 \div 8 =$
$30 \div 6 =$	$81 \div 9 =$	$21 \div 3 =$	$81 \div 9 =$
$10 \div 5 =$	$56 \div 8 =$	$100 \div 10 =$	$8 \div 1 =$
$24 \div 6 =$	$14 \div 2 =$	$12 \div 3 =$	$0 \div 9 =$
$16 \div 2 =$	$0 \div 1 =$	$90 \div 10 =$	$10 \div 5 =$

Time: _____   Score: _____

12 ÷ 6 =	0 ÷ 1 =	2 ÷ 1 =	4 ÷ 1 =
40 ÷ 10 =	28 ÷ 7 =	8 ÷ 8 =	12 ÷ 2 =
2 ÷ 2 =	2 ÷ 2 =	50 ÷ 5 =	63 ÷ 9 =
10 ÷ 5 =	8 ÷ 2 =	81 ÷ 9 =	3 ÷ 1 =
8 ÷ 1 =	12 ÷ 2 =	10 ÷ 2 =	28 ÷ 4 =
0 ÷ 2 =	90 ÷ 10 =	0 ÷ 2 =	49 ÷ 7 =
60 ÷ 10 =	8 ÷ 4 =	18 ÷ 9 =	50 ÷ 5 =
20 ÷ 2 =	18 ÷ 6 =	48 ÷ 6 =	6 ÷ 1 =
24 ÷ 4 =	48 ÷ 8 =	5 ÷ 1 =	8 ÷ 4 =
6 ÷ 1 =	6 ÷ 2 =	24 ÷ 6 =	24 ÷ 3 =
2 ÷ 2 =	80 ÷ 8 =	3 ÷ 1 =	90 ÷ 9 =
15 ÷ 3 =	24 ÷ 4 =	35 ÷ 7 =	50 ÷ 5 =
90 ÷ 9 =	12 ÷ 3 =	100 ÷ 10 =	7 ÷ 7 =
21 ÷ 7 =	56 ÷ 8 =	12 ÷ 3 =	0 ÷ 8 =
36 ÷ 9 =	6 ÷ 3 =	18 ÷ 6 =	72 ÷ 9 =
20 ÷ 10 =	49 ÷ 7 =	50 ÷ 5 =	9 ÷ 9 =
63 ÷ 7 =	30 ÷ 5 =	81 ÷ 9 =	18 ÷ 3 =
0 ÷ 7 =	72 ÷ 8 =	14 ÷ 7 =	24 ÷ 6 =

Time: _____   Score: _____

$72 \div 9 =$	$63 \div 7 =$	$16 \div 2 =$	$8 \div 4 =$
$24 \div 8 =$	$56 \div 7 =$	$72 \div 9 =$	$63 \div 9 =$
$35 \div 7 =$	$14 \div 2 =$	$36 \div 6 =$	$40 \div 4 =$
$0 \div 7 =$	$18 \div 6 =$	$70 \div 7 =$	$8 \div 4 =$
$48 \div 6 =$	$4 \div 2 =$	$63 \div 7 =$	$10 \div 5 =$
$28 \div 7 =$	$20 \div 10 =$	$36 \div 4 =$	$50 \div 5 =$
$16 \div 2 =$	$35 \div 5 =$	$20 \div 5 =$	$12 \div 6 =$
$14 \div 7 =$	$36 \div 4 =$	$28 \div 4 =$	$20 \div 5 =$
$27 \div 9 =$	$32 \div 4 =$	$54 \div 9 =$	$24 \div 6 =$
$56 \div 7 =$	$18 \div 6 =$	$32 \div 4 =$	$20 \div 4 =$
$60 \div 6 =$	$72 \div 9 =$	$70 \div 10 =$	$7 \div 1 =$
$56 \div 7 =$	$40 \div 5 =$	$63 \div 7 =$	$3 \div 3 =$
$60 \div 10 =$	$8 \div 1 =$	$40 \div 4 =$	$2 \div 2 =$
$90 \div 10 =$	$30 \div 6 =$	$9 \div 9 =$	$24 \div 8 =$
$12 \div 2 =$	$8 \div 4 =$	$36 \div 4 =$	$16 \div 8 =$
$40 \div 4 =$	$0 \div 4 =$	$4 \div 2 =$	$27 \div 9 =$
$8 \div 2 =$	$14 \div 7 =$	$42 \div 7 =$	$49 \div 7 =$
$18 \div 3 =$	$2 \div 1 =$	$81 \div 9 =$	$30 \div 6 =$

Time: _____   Score: _____

$30 \div 5 =$	$25 \div 5 =$	$54 \div 9 =$	$30 \div 10 =$
$16 \div 8 =$	$25 \div 5 =$	$35 \div 5 =$	$20 \div 2 =$
$16 \div 8 =$	$49 \div 7 =$	$32 \div 8 =$	$20 \div 2 =$
$14 \div 2 =$	$12 \div 6 =$	$10 \div 1 =$	$0 \div 10 =$
$1 \div 1 =$	$40 \div 10 =$	$12 \div 3 =$	$9 \div 3 =$
$40 \div 8 =$	$15 \div 5 =$	$48 \div 8 =$	$0 \div 4 =$
$8 \div 1 =$	$14 \div 7 =$	$6 \div 3 =$	$7 \div 7 =$
$36 \div 9 =$	$20 \div 5 =$	$0 \div 4 =$	$60 \div 6 =$
$80 \div 10 =$	$30 \div 3 =$	$72 \div 8 =$	$54 \div 9 =$
$50 \div 5 =$	$40 \div 10 =$	$40 \div 10 =$	$90 \div 10 =$
$24 \div 8 =$	$30 \div 6 =$	$24 \div 6 =$	$24 \div 4 =$
$16 \div 4 =$	$63 \div 9 =$	$90 \div 10 =$	$100 \div 10 =$
$12 \div 3 =$	$6 \div 1 =$	$70 \div 7 =$	$18 \div 2 =$
$18 \div 3 =$	$18 \div 6 =$	$42 \div 7 =$	$90 \div 10 =$
$24 \div 8 =$	$20 \div 10 =$	$3 \div 1 =$	$6 \div 1 =$
$5 \div 1 =$	$18 \div 9 =$	$0 \div 5 =$	$3 \div 1 =$
$4 \div 2 =$	$0 \div 7 =$	$12 \div 3 =$	$8 \div 2 =$
$8 \div 4 =$	$90 \div 9 =$	$24 \div 3 =$	$0 \div 3 =$

Time: _____   Score: _____

$7 \div 1 =$	$18 \div 9 =$	$0 \div 10 =$	$48 \div 6 =$
$12 \div 2 =$	$12 \div 4 =$	$36 \div 4 =$	$15 \div 3 =$
$14 \div 7 =$	$6 \div 2 =$	$3 \div 3 =$	$0 \div 2 =$
$32 \div 4 =$	$1 \div 1 =$	$15 \div 3 =$	$24 \div 4 =$
$0 \div 7 =$	$8 \div 8 =$	$60 \div 6 =$	$27 \div 9 =$
$0 \div 9 =$	$20 \div 10 =$	$24 \div 3 =$	$12 \div 6 =$
$16 \div 4 =$	$18 \div 3 =$	$18 \div 2 =$	$18 \div 3 =$
$7 \div 1 =$	$7 \div 7 =$	$12 \div 3 =$	$63 \div 9 =$
$45 \div 9 =$	$15 \div 5 =$	$56 \div 8 =$	$24 \div 6 =$
$8 \div 1 =$	$40 \div 4 =$	$12 \div 3 =$	$72 \div 9 =$
$2 \div 1 =$	$30 \div 10 =$	$54 \div 9 =$	$90 \div 10 =$
$24 \div 4 =$	$54 \div 9 =$	$0 \div 10 =$	$12 \div 2 =$
$6 \div 2 =$	$12 \div 2 =$	$72 \div 8 =$	$0 \div 10 =$
$36 \div 9 =$	$16 \div 8 =$	$5 \div 5 =$	$6 \div 2 =$
$14 \div 7 =$	$50 \div 5 =$	$8 \div 1 =$	$80 \div 10 =$
$60 \div 10 =$	$0 \div 4 =$	$9 \div 3 =$	$20 \div 5 =$
$70 \div 10 =$	$10 \div 2 =$	$21 \div 3 =$	$42 \div 7 =$
$40 \div 8 =$	$70 \div 7 =$	$18 \div 9 =$	$10 \div 1 =$

Time: _____   Score: _____

$7 \div 7 =$	$9 \div 1 =$	$60 \div 6 =$	$36 \div 6 =$
$8 \div 2 =$	$6 \div 1 =$	$60 \div 6 =$	$0 \div 10 =$
$50 \div 10 =$	$0 \div 9 =$	$80 \div 8 =$	$54 \div 6 =$
$42 \div 6 =$	$5 \div 1 =$	$16 \div 4 =$	$12 \div 6 =$
$48 \div 6 =$	$15 \div 3 =$	$2 \div 1 =$	$42 \div 6 =$
$72 \div 8 =$	$45 \div 9 =$	$0 \div 4 =$	$6 \div 2 =$
$35 \div 5 =$	$35 \div 7 =$	$4 \div 2 =$	$36 \div 9 =$
$56 \div 7 =$	$42 \div 6 =$	$50 \div 10 =$	$49 \div 7 =$
$4 \div 2 =$	$60 \div 10 =$	$7 \div 7 =$	$30 \div 5 =$
$30 \div 10 =$	$54 \div 9 =$	$6 \div 3 =$	$3 \div 3 =$
$60 \div 6 =$	$8 \div 1 =$	$25 \div 5 =$	$9 \div 9 =$
$27 \div 3 =$	$56 \div 8 =$	$48 \div 6 =$	$9 \div 9 =$
$12 \div 3 =$	$6 \div 3 =$	$10 \div 5 =$	$7 \div 1 =$
$70 \div 10 =$	$8 \div 8 =$	$45 \div 5 =$	$6 \div 3 =$
$20 \div 5 =$	$24 \div 4 =$	$10 \div 10 =$	$18 \div 2 =$
$35 \div 5 =$	$21 \div 7 =$	$24 \div 6 =$	$14 \div 2 =$
$90 \div 9 =$	$6 \div 3 =$	$9 \div 9 =$	$3 \div 1 =$
$63 \div 9 =$	$36 \div 6 =$	$27 \div 9 =$	$24 \div 8 =$

Time: _____   Score: _____

8 ÷ 8 =	63 ÷ 9 =	1 ÷ 1 =	1 ÷ 1 =
70 ÷ 10 =	4 ÷ 2 =	70 ÷ 7 =	8 ÷ 4 =
6 ÷ 2 =	40 ÷ 8 =	18 ÷ 3 =	63 ÷ 9 =
0 ÷ 10 =	4 ÷ 1 =	5 ÷ 1 =	30 ÷ 6 =
30 ÷ 3 =	42 ÷ 6 =	8 ÷ 8 =	28 ÷ 7 =
80 ÷ 10 =	50 ÷ 10 =	2 ÷ 2 =	0 ÷ 7 =
36 ÷ 4 =	10 ÷ 2 =	0 ÷ 5 =	8 ÷ 4 =
7 ÷ 1 =	0 ÷ 6 =	4 ÷ 4 =	21 ÷ 7 =
70 ÷ 10 =	63 ÷ 9 =	72 ÷ 8 =	0 ÷ 8 =
0 ÷ 2 =	3 ÷ 3 =	54 ÷ 6 =	56 ÷ 7 =
28 ÷ 4 =	63 ÷ 7 =	35 ÷ 7 =	20 ÷ 2 =
9 ÷ 9 =	63 ÷ 7 =	24 ÷ 3 =	9 ÷ 9 =
0 ÷ 7 =	20 ÷ 2 =	8 ÷ 8 =	24 ÷ 6 =
40 ÷ 5 =	2 ÷ 2 =	12 ÷ 4 =	32 ÷ 8 =
8 ÷ 4 =	6 ÷ 3 =	48 ÷ 8 =	16 ÷ 2 =
14 ÷ 7 =	9 ÷ 3 =	30 ÷ 10 =	30 ÷ 5 =
36 ÷ 4 =	45 ÷ 9 =	24 ÷ 8 =	48 ÷ 6 =
28 ÷ 4 =	64 ÷ 8 =	25 ÷ 5 =	56 ÷ 7 =

Time: _____   Score: _____

$12 \div 4 =$	$70 \div 10 =$	$60 \div 10 =$	$0 \div 8 =$
$40 \div 4 =$	$6 \div 2 =$	$45 \div 5 =$	$24 \div 4 =$
$12 \div 2 =$	$0 \div 5 =$	$10 \div 5 =$	$9 \div 3 =$
$70 \div 10 =$	$70 \div 7 =$	$63 \div 9 =$	$7 \div 7 =$
$48 \div 6 =$	$63 \div 9 =$	$48 \div 8 =$	$80 \div 8 =$
$100 \div 10 =$	$50 \div 5 =$	$8 \div 4 =$	$24 \div 4 =$
$24 \div 4 =$	$12 \div 6 =$	$48 \div 6 =$	$4 \div 2 =$
$8 \div 2 =$	$8 \div 4 =$	$81 \div 9 =$	$56 \div 7 =$
$8 \div 8 =$	$0 \div 3 =$	$49 \div 7 =$	$42 \div 7 =$
$24 \div 4 =$	$70 \div 10 =$	$0 \div 9 =$	$4 \div 4 =$
$6 \div 6 =$	$36 \div 6 =$	$48 \div 6 =$	$28 \div 4 =$
$50 \div 10 =$	$4 \div 1 =$	$72 \div 8 =$	$14 \div 7 =$
$100 \div 10 =$	$18 \div 6 =$	$4 \div 2 =$	$6 \div 2 =$
$0 \div 4 =$	$40 \div 10 =$	$80 \div 10 =$	$30 \div 6 =$
$14 \div 7 =$	$16 \div 2 =$	$3 \div 3 =$	$27 \div 3 =$
$3 \div 3 =$	$15 \div 3 =$	$25 \div 5 =$	$5 \div 5 =$
$18 \div 9 =$	$27 \div 3 =$	$21 \div 7 =$	$8 \div 1 =$
$2 \div 1 =$	$54 \div 6 =$	$6 \div 6 =$	$28 \div 4 =$

Time: _____   Score: _____

5 ÷ 1 =	60 ÷ 10 =	20 ÷ 2 =	18 ÷ 6 =
0 ÷ 6 =	63 ÷ 9 =	56 ÷ 7 =	12 ÷ 2 =
30 ÷ 6 =	30 ÷ 3 =	12 ÷ 2 =	49 ÷ 7 =
18 ÷ 6 =	24 ÷ 6 =	32 ÷ 8 =	15 ÷ 5 =
54 ÷ 9 =	5 ÷ 1 =	48 ÷ 8 =	14 ÷ 7 =
60 ÷ 6 =	60 ÷ 6 =	36 ÷ 9 =	0 ÷ 5 =
48 ÷ 8 =	72 ÷ 9 =	18 ÷ 2 =	10 ÷ 2 =
12 ÷ 4 =	0 ÷ 4 =	27 ÷ 3 =	60 ÷ 6 =
24 ÷ 6 =	63 ÷ 9 =	50 ÷ 10 =	32 ÷ 4 =
8 ÷ 2 =	4 ÷ 4 =	18 ÷ 2 =	40 ÷ 5 =
10 ÷ 1 =	21 ÷ 3 =	54 ÷ 6 =	28 ÷ 7 =
32 ÷ 4 =	9 ÷ 3 =	3 ÷ 1 =	21 ÷ 7 =
16 ÷ 4 =	20 ÷ 4 =	70 ÷ 7 =	6 ÷ 2 =
10 ÷ 1 =	0 ÷ 6 =	36 ÷ 4 =	60 ÷ 10 =
12 ÷ 6 =	72 ÷ 9 =	25 ÷ 5 =	4 ÷ 4 =
45 ÷ 9 =	16 ÷ 2 =	32 ÷ 4 =	90 ÷ 10 =
1 ÷ 1 =	32 ÷ 4 =	18 ÷ 6 =	54 ÷ 6 =
0 ÷ 4 =	36 ÷ 9 =	49 ÷ 7 =	60 ÷ 10 =

Time: _____   Score: _____

$8 \div 4 =$	$90 \div 9 =$	$50 \div 5 =$	$3 \div 1 =$
$6 \div 2 =$	$8 \div 2 =$	$36 \div 6 =$	$28 \div 4 =$
$60 \div 10 =$	$15 \div 5 =$	$16 \div 8 =$	$16 \div 4 =$
$20 \div 2 =$	$56 \div 8 =$	$14 \div 7 =$	$20 \div 4 =$
$32 \div 8 =$	$9 \div 3 =$	$56 \div 8 =$	$24 \div 4 =$
$70 \div 7 =$	$28 \div 4 =$	$24 \div 8 =$	$7 \div 7 =$
$16 \div 4 =$	$12 \div 6 =$	$0 \div 3 =$	$10 \div 10 =$
$56 \div 8 =$	$40 \div 10 =$	$7 \div 7 =$	$56 \div 7 =$
$21 \div 7 =$	$81 \div 9 =$	$15 \div 3 =$	$0 \div 7 =$
$4 \div 2 =$	$40 \div 8 =$	$8 \div 1 =$	$3 \div 1 =$
$16 \div 8 =$	$27 \div 9 =$	$16 \div 4 =$	$32 \div 8 =$
$0 \div 1 =$	$9 \div 9 =$	$6 \div 2 =$	$100 \div 10 =$
$25 \div 5 =$	$14 \div 2 =$	$5 \div 1 =$	$63 \div 9 =$
$100 \div 10 =$	$30 \div 10 =$	$50 \div 5 =$	$2 \div 1 =$
$9 \div 9 =$	$40 \div 8 =$	$18 \div 9 =$	$4 \div 2 =$
$72 \div 8 =$	$2 \div 1 =$	$0 \div 10 =$	$2 \div 1 =$
$42 \div 7 =$	$18 \div 3 =$	$0 \div 1 =$	$49 \div 7 =$
$49 \div 7 =$	$60 \div 6 =$	$6 \div 3 =$	$36 \div 9 =$

Time: _____   Score: _____

24 ÷ 8 =	28 ÷ 4 =	36 ÷ 6 =	56 ÷ 7 =
35 ÷ 5 =	60 ÷ 10 =	20 ÷ 10 =	40 ÷ 10 =
12 ÷ 3 =	3 ÷ 3 =	14 ÷ 2 =	45 ÷ 5 =
10 ÷ 2 =	45 ÷ 9 =	8 ÷ 2 =	6 ÷ 2 =
42 ÷ 7 =	54 ÷ 9 =	70 ÷ 7 =	8 ÷ 2 =
9 ÷ 9 =	8 ÷ 2 =	56 ÷ 7 =	10 ÷ 1 =
6 ÷ 3 =	16 ÷ 2 =	4 ÷ 2 =	48 ÷ 6 =
90 ÷ 9 =	70 ÷ 10 =	7 ÷ 1 =	24 ÷ 8 =
6 ÷ 6 =	9 ÷ 1 =	25 ÷ 5 =	100 ÷ 10 =
42 ÷ 7 =	12 ÷ 2 =	42 ÷ 6 =	90 ÷ 10 =
80 ÷ 8 =	40 ÷ 5 =	49 ÷ 7 =	24 ÷ 6 =
18 ÷ 6 =	56 ÷ 8 =	15 ÷ 5 =	48 ÷ 6 =
0 ÷ 10 =	0 ÷ 8 =	54 ÷ 6 =	12 ÷ 6 =
60 ÷ 6 =	2 ÷ 2 =	30 ÷ 6 =	0 ÷ 2 =
4 ÷ 1 =	60 ÷ 10 =	25 ÷ 5 =	21 ÷ 3 =
10 ÷ 5 =	9 ÷ 9 =	0 ÷ 9 =	24 ÷ 3 =
60 ÷ 10 =	25 ÷ 5 =	15 ÷ 3 =	50 ÷ 5 =
6 ÷ 1 =	0 ÷ 1 =	4 ÷ 4 =	60 ÷ 10 =

Time: _____   Score: _____

$5 \div 5 =$	$20 \div 2 =$	$40 \div 5 =$	$10 \div 10 =$
$0 \div 5 =$	$30 \div 5 =$	$18 \div 2 =$	$90 \div 10 =$
$0 \div 9 =$	$0 \div 2 =$	$60 \div 10 =$	$27 \div 9 =$
$49 \div 7 =$	$18 \div 6 =$	$9 \div 9 =$	$25 \div 5 =$
$27 \div 9 =$	$8 \div 2 =$	$36 \div 9 =$	$0 \div 6 =$
$70 \div 10 =$	$36 \div 9 =$	$81 \div 9 =$	$6 \div 1 =$
$9 \div 1 =$	$30 \div 10 =$	$80 \div 10 =$	$60 \div 10 =$
$6 \div 1 =$	$48 \div 8 =$	$20 \div 4 =$	$0 \div 6 =$
$18 \div 3 =$	$63 \div 7 =$	$10 \div 10 =$	$9 \div 3 =$
$27 \div 3 =$	$20 \div 4 =$	$64 \div 8 =$	$20 \div 2 =$
$56 \div 7 =$	$0 \div 7 =$	$63 \div 7 =$	$18 \div 6 =$
$60 \div 6 =$	$14 \div 7 =$	$27 \div 9 =$	$5 \div 1 =$
$90 \div 9 =$	$6 \div 1 =$	$5 \div 1 =$	$72 \div 8 =$
$0 \div 7 =$	$6 \div 1 =$	$70 \div 7 =$	$0 \div 3 =$
$80 \div 10 =$	$16 \div 4 =$	$18 \div 6 =$	$36 \div 9 =$
$40 \div 10 =$	$54 \div 6 =$	$0 \div 3 =$	$28 \div 7 =$
$36 \div 6 =$	$28 \div 7 =$	$30 \div 5 =$	$2 \div 1 =$
$10 \div 2 =$	$56 \div 8 =$	$0 \div 6 =$	$54 \div 6 =$

Time: _____   Score: _____

16 ÷ 8 =	18 ÷ 2 =	28 ÷ 7 =	0 ÷ 2 =
14 ÷ 2 =	21 ÷ 7 =	15 ÷ 3 =	8 ÷ 8 =
15 ÷ 3 =	63 ÷ 9 =	21 ÷ 3 =	4 ÷ 1 =
63 ÷ 9 =	9 ÷ 9 =	20 ÷ 10 =	30 ÷ 10 =
45 ÷ 9 =	28 ÷ 7 =	10 ÷ 1 =	40 ÷ 8 =
35 ÷ 7 =	27 ÷ 9 =	100 ÷ 10 =	16 ÷ 4 =
6 ÷ 3 =	40 ÷ 10 =	72 ÷ 9 =	72 ÷ 8 =
20 ÷ 4 =	35 ÷ 7 =	5 ÷ 5 =	24 ÷ 3 =
25 ÷ 5 =	36 ÷ 6 =	18 ÷ 6 =	7 ÷ 7 =
35 ÷ 7 =	10 ÷ 2 =	7 ÷ 1 =	70 ÷ 7 =
15 ÷ 5 =	30 ÷ 3 =	20 ÷ 5 =	4 ÷ 2 =
48 ÷ 6 =	9 ÷ 9 =	0 ÷ 9 =	4 ÷ 4 =
50 ÷ 5 =	45 ÷ 9 =	48 ÷ 8 =	30 ÷ 5 =
72 ÷ 9 =	50 ÷ 10 =	10 ÷ 5 =	9 ÷ 1 =
27 ÷ 9 =	63 ÷ 7 =	1 ÷ 1 =	64 ÷ 8 =
20 ÷ 4 =	72 ÷ 8 =	0 ÷ 1 =	50 ÷ 10 =
30 ÷ 5 =	25 ÷ 5 =	72 ÷ 9 =	36 ÷ 6 =
12 ÷ 3 =	7 ÷ 7 =	42 ÷ 6 =	10 ÷ 1 =

Time: _____   Score: _____

36 ÷ 9 =	28 ÷ 4 =	7 ÷ 7 =	63 ÷ 9 =
48 ÷ 6 =	20 ÷ 10 =	18 ÷ 9 =	10 ÷ 10 =
6 ÷ 2 =	14 ÷ 7 =	5 ÷ 1 =	35 ÷ 5 =
1 ÷ 1 =	20 ÷ 10 =	20 ÷ 4 =	56 ÷ 8 =
54 ÷ 9 =	56 ÷ 8 =	6 ÷ 3 =	14 ÷ 2 =
20 ÷ 4 =	32 ÷ 8 =	20 ÷ 10 =	90 ÷ 10 =
42 ÷ 7 =	9 ÷ 3 =	24 ÷ 3 =	63 ÷ 7 =
42 ÷ 7 =	27 ÷ 3 =	21 ÷ 3 =	81 ÷ 9 =
28 ÷ 4 =	12 ÷ 6 =	27 ÷ 9 =	21 ÷ 7 =
21 ÷ 3 =	63 ÷ 9 =	6 ÷ 1 =	45 ÷ 5 =
0 ÷ 2 =	0 ÷ 1 =	90 ÷ 10 =	90 ÷ 10 =
12 ÷ 6 =	24 ÷ 6 =	9 ÷ 9 =	72 ÷ 8 =
0 ÷ 5 =	16 ÷ 8 =	4 ÷ 4 =	0 ÷ 1 =
54 ÷ 9 =	32 ÷ 8 =	80 ÷ 10 =	56 ÷ 7 =
45 ÷ 5 =	63 ÷ 9 =	27 ÷ 3 =	0 ÷ 9 =
40 ÷ 8 =	48 ÷ 8 =	64 ÷ 8 =	48 ÷ 6 =
30 ÷ 10 =	12 ÷ 6 =	24 ÷ 3 =	4 ÷ 1 =
15 ÷ 5 =	42 ÷ 6 =	28 ÷ 7 =	21 ÷ 7 =

Time: _____   Score: _____

36 ÷ 6 =	30 ÷ 10 =	49 ÷ 7 =	70 ÷ 10 =
0 ÷ 6 =	24 ÷ 4 =	81 ÷ 9 =	25 ÷ 5 =
6 ÷ 3 =	12 ÷ 4 =	10 ÷ 2 =	63 ÷ 9 =
6 ÷ 2 =	3 ÷ 3 =	4 ÷ 2 =	28 ÷ 4 =
6 ÷ 2 =	42 ÷ 6 =	0 ÷ 1 =	30 ÷ 6 =
16 ÷ 4 =	0 ÷ 7 =	18 ÷ 9 =	7 ÷ 7 =
49 ÷ 7 =	40 ÷ 10 =	28 ÷ 7 =	28 ÷ 4 =
18 ÷ 9 =	90 ÷ 10 =	10 ÷ 2 =	20 ÷ 5 =
5 ÷ 1 =	40 ÷ 8 =	90 ÷ 10 =	18 ÷ 6 =
80 ÷ 8 =	21 ÷ 7 =	16 ÷ 4 =	48 ÷ 6 =
40 ÷ 5 =	80 ÷ 10 =	4 ÷ 2 =	63 ÷ 7 =
45 ÷ 5 =	50 ÷ 5 =	90 ÷ 10 =	2 ÷ 1 =
8 ÷ 8 =	27 ÷ 3 =	30 ÷ 10 =	9 ÷ 9 =
81 ÷ 9 =	30 ÷ 6 =	63 ÷ 9 =	0 ÷ 9 =
3 ÷ 1 =	80 ÷ 10 =	30 ÷ 3 =	0 ÷ 9 =
100 ÷ 10 =	27 ÷ 3 =	12 ÷ 3 =	0 ÷ 7 =
36 ÷ 4 =	40 ÷ 10 =	60 ÷ 6 =	50 ÷ 5 =
63 ÷ 7 =	16 ÷ 4 =	24 ÷ 4 =	3 ÷ 3 =

Time: _____   Score: _____

$2 \div 1 =$	$20 \div 4 =$	$25 \div 5 =$	$21 \div 3 =$
$30 \div 10 =$	$30 \div 5 =$	$50 \div 5 =$	$0 \div 1 =$
$18 \div 3 =$	$25 \div 5 =$	$18 \div 9 =$	$80 \div 8 =$
$27 \div 9 =$	$0 \div 3 =$	$24 \div 8 =$	$35 \div 7 =$
$35 \div 5 =$	$5 \div 1 =$	$21 \div 3 =$	$81 \div 9 =$
$28 \div 4 =$	$28 \div 4 =$	$50 \div 10 =$	$70 \div 10 =$
$0 \div 5 =$	$10 \div 5 =$	$0 \div 10 =$	$18 \div 6 =$
$36 \div 9 =$	$28 \div 4 =$	$2 \div 1 =$	$9 \div 1 =$
$16 \div 4 =$	$8 \div 4 =$	$30 \div 10 =$	$0 \div 3 =$
$49 \div 7 =$	$12 \div 2 =$	$42 \div 6 =$	$12 \div 4 =$
$0 \div 8 =$	$3 \div 3 =$	$4 \div 1 =$	$25 \div 5 =$
$72 \div 9 =$	$72 \div 9 =$	$14 \div 7 =$	$12 \div 2 =$
$5 \div 1 =$	$35 \div 5 =$	$36 \div 4 =$	$48 \div 8 =$
$6 \div 6 =$	$25 \div 5 =$	$15 \div 5 =$	$0 \div 7 =$
$0 \div 7 =$	$0 \div 4 =$	$10 \div 1 =$	$50 \div 5 =$
$2 \div 2 =$	$35 \div 7 =$	$4 \div 1 =$	$35 \div 7 =$
$0 \div 6 =$	$56 \div 8 =$	$30 \div 10 =$	$18 \div 6 =$
$2 \div 2 =$	$7 \div 1 =$	$10 \div 10 =$	$20 \div 2 =$

Time: _____   Score: _____

42 ÷ 6 =	18 ÷ 2 =	20 ÷ 4 =	56 ÷ 8 =
14 ÷ 2 =	70 ÷ 7 =	24 ÷ 6 =	80 ÷ 8 =
0 ÷ 10 =	0 ÷ 9 =	27 ÷ 9 =	4 ÷ 4 =
30 ÷ 10 =	100 ÷ 10 =	0 ÷ 1 =	70 ÷ 7 =
30 ÷ 6 =	15 ÷ 5 =	2 ÷ 1 =	32 ÷ 4 =
42 ÷ 7 =	40 ÷ 10 =	20 ÷ 4 =	60 ÷ 6 =
16 ÷ 2 =	24 ÷ 6 =	49 ÷ 7 =	4 ÷ 2 =
3 ÷ 3 =	10 ÷ 1 =	16 ÷ 2 =	16 ÷ 8 =
40 ÷ 10 =	18 ÷ 3 =	20 ÷ 4 =	45 ÷ 9 =
12 ÷ 6 =	35 ÷ 5 =	21 ÷ 3 =	24 ÷ 3 =
60 ÷ 10 =	28 ÷ 7 =	70 ÷ 7 =	20 ÷ 10 =
18 ÷ 9 =	49 ÷ 7 =	3 ÷ 1 =	42 ÷ 6 =
42 ÷ 7 =	25 ÷ 5 =	14 ÷ 2 =	0 ÷ 8 =
4 ÷ 4 =	10 ÷ 5 =	0 ÷ 8 =	70 ÷ 7 =
32 ÷ 4 =	18 ÷ 3 =	20 ÷ 2 =	70 ÷ 7 =
10 ÷ 5 =	30 ÷ 5 =	36 ÷ 4 =	16 ÷ 8 =
60 ÷ 10 =	0 ÷ 3 =	30 ÷ 5 =	27 ÷ 3 =
42 ÷ 6 =	1 ÷ 1 =	0 ÷ 5 =	5 ÷ 1 =

Time: _____   Score: _____

72 ÷ 8 =	9 ÷ 3 =	63 ÷ 9 =	10 ÷ 10 =
9 ÷ 1 =	49 ÷ 7 =	18 ÷ 3 =	20 ÷ 5 =
35 ÷ 7 =	8 ÷ 4 =	16 ÷ 2 =	0 ÷ 6 =
35 ÷ 5 =	60 ÷ 6 =	14 ÷ 7 =	2 ÷ 2 =
21 ÷ 7 =	35 ÷ 5 =	0 ÷ 5 =	48 ÷ 6 =
7 ÷ 7 =	9 ÷ 9 =	14 ÷ 2 =	60 ÷ 10 =
0 ÷ 7 =	2 ÷ 2 =	24 ÷ 8 =	1 ÷ 1 =
24 ÷ 6 =	16 ÷ 8 =	3 ÷ 1 =	90 ÷ 9 =
24 ÷ 3 =	24 ÷ 6 =	9 ÷ 9 =	2 ÷ 2 =
30 ÷ 5 =	8 ÷ 1 =	28 ÷ 4 =	2 ÷ 2 =
0 ÷ 1 =	70 ÷ 7 =	16 ÷ 8 =	6 ÷ 1 =
42 ÷ 6 =	0 ÷ 3 =	25 ÷ 5 =	63 ÷ 7 =
14 ÷ 7 =	36 ÷ 6 =	7 ÷ 1 =	18 ÷ 3 =
0 ÷ 8 =	28 ÷ 4 =	45 ÷ 9 =	8 ÷ 8 =
14 ÷ 7 =	40 ÷ 5 =	18 ÷ 3 =	15 ÷ 3 =
30 ÷ 3 =	27 ÷ 3 =	0 ÷ 6 =	36 ÷ 4 =
80 ÷ 10 =	72 ÷ 8 =	0 ÷ 7 =	49 ÷ 7 =
100 ÷ 10 =	6 ÷ 6 =	40 ÷ 4 =	60 ÷ 10 =

CPSIA information can be obtained at www.ICGtesting.com
Printed in the USA
LVOW031509150212

268849LV00001B/27/P